Pamela grew up on the coast south of Adelaide and trained as a lab technician in the Royal Adelaide Hospital before moving to Sydney in her early twenties. Wanderlust drove her to her first long overseas trip in the seventies, and even now every year finds her somewhere on the trail, usually with a backpack.

After a few years away, Pamela returned to Adelaide to do an Arts degree at Flinders University before going back to laboratory work.

She now lives on the northern beaches in Sydney where she had a career change and taught English as a Second Language to health professionals.

Now retired, she spends her days writing, bushwalking, kayaking, bike-riding, bush-regenerating and on penguin watch around Manly..

Surviving the Seventies

©

Pamela Irving

First published by Pamela Irving in 2020
This edition published in 2020 by Pamela Irving

Copyright © Pamela Irving 2020
The moral right of the author has been asserted.

All rights reserved. This publication (or any part of it) may not be reproduced or transmitted, copied, stored, distributed or otherwise made available by any person or entity (including Google, Amazon or similar organisations), in any form (electronic, digital, optical, mechanical) or by any means (photocopying, recording, scanning or otherwise) without prior written permission from the publisher.

Surviving the Seventies

EPUB: 9781925786965
POD: 9781925786972

Cover design by Red Tally Studios

Publishing services provided by Critical Mass
www.critmassconsulting.com

A stone's throw out on either hand
From that well-ordered road we tread
And all the world is wild and strange.

In The House of Suddhoo
By Rudyard Kipling

I'm running down the footpath beside Blues Point Road in North Sydney. I'm shaking violently. My heart is beating through my chest. Every cell of my body is bursting with terror. It's after midnight in the middle of winter. The street is deserted.

I can hear his footsteps gaining on me. I'm wearing shoes with two-inch chunky heels. Not stilettos, thank God, but running shoes they aren't. I feel his hand clamp my shoulder, and I'm thrown on to the road.

We are outside a block of flats and I break away and run inside up the stairs. He catches me on a landing and pulls me to the ground. I am screaming to waken the dead but the doors of the flats remain tightly closed.

He pulls me back to the footpath. I look around in desperation but the street remains empty. He tries to drag me back to the car but at five feet eight I'm not much shorter than he is, and he isn't strong enough to carry me.

A car pulls into the parking area, spotlighting the road. Hope pushes terror aside. I scream for help.

I get up and run to the car. My right ankle keeps collapsing. My shoe is loose, trailing flimsy ribbon ties.

I am aware of my assailant running back to his car parked at an angle in the middle of the road, its headlights still shining, the driver's door wide open.

Chapter 1

"I've just had a terrible fight with my boyfriend. I've got to get to Epping. Can you take me?" I sob through my saviour's open window. The startled face of the driver, a conservative-looking man in his mid-forties, stares back at me. "Just wait here a minute."

He parks the car and disappears into the building. I assume he's gone to explain to his wife this drama he's got himself caught up in. When he comes back down, I get into the car and we set off for Epping.

I explain the bare bones of my predicament. "We had a fight. He's got a terrible temper."

We continue along for a minute or two in silence. "Would you like to have a cup of coffee somewhere?" he asks.

"No, I've got to get to my friends' place. It's late. They'll already be in bed." Anxiety at waking Hans and Heather so late is rising up in me.

A couple more minutes of silence follow. The car has bench seats, not the two separate front seats of later cars. He pats the seat next to him. "Do you want to move over next to me?"

I've never been able to think on my feet but my guardian angel steps in for the second time that night. "Stop the car, stop the car. I feel sick. I'm going to be sick."

He wrenches the car to the curb and before it stops I am outside on the footpath.

"Thanks for the lift," I say as I slam the door. My rescuer-cum-molester rapidly turns the car around and speeds off back the way we came.

I'm on the side of a major road and it's pitch black. I have no idea where I am. There are no cars coming in either direction, but I'm not about to repeat the last episode anyway. I look up and down the road. Shall I start walking? In which direction? Shall I hide somewhere and wait until morning?

As I stand, my mind a blank, in steps my angel again. A taxi approaches from behind. In no time I'm in the doorway in front of the bewildered Hans and Heather, garbling my explanation between tears. Heather has to write a cheque for the taxi driver. Everything I own is back with Ken in his boarding house.

Surviving the Seventies

*

Self-preservation kicked in. I went to a CHUMS meeting: Care and Help for Unmarried Mothers. The politically incorrect name of the group mildly embarrassed me then. Now it makes me wince. However, unfortunate labels aside, it turned out a god-send. How had I, this well-raised, well-educated, conservative Adelaide girl ended up in Sydney, a penniless single mother, the victim of domestic violence?

The stories of the other young women in the group fascinated me. They were in their teens, twenties and thirties, and from right across the social spectrum. I started to feel not so alone. I told my own story, how I'd met Ken, a sailor just back from Vietnam, at a summer wedding in Adelaide. He'd been good fun, in party mood after months in Asia on the ship. He had a great smile, beautiful white even teeth and curly dark hair which fell across his brow. Exotic, with an Indonesian father. I wasn't particularly looking for a permanent partner – I was finishing my course in Medical Technology and had plans to sail to England the next year.

Ken, however, was ready to settle down. His own childhood had been traumatic. His mother had left his violent father and Ken ended up in a Salvation Army Boys' Home, considered uncontrollable. His two previous relationships had ended with the girls leaving him, and he was determined the same thing wouldn't happen with me. Our relationship was conducted between Adelaide and Sydney where Ken's ship, the *HMAS Brisbane*, was based. It was a novelty to have an interstate boyfriend. We drove back to Sydney together on one occasion – it was a buzz to see the Harbour Bridge as we arrived at dawn. I wore a long white gown with small black polka dots to the *Brisbane* annual ball. I caught the bus to Melbourne, Ken drove, and together we explored the city. My housemates and I met Ken in Canberra and we drove around admiring the mansions housing international diplomats.

Ken was due to go back to Vietnam the following March, and I planned to go to England that April. I vaguely imagined we'd meet up sometime when his tour of duty finished, and see how things went then. I knew his feelings for me were stronger than mine for him, but I was just going with the flow, letting the universe take care of things. I was living in a share-house with three friends and – what with work, study, relationships and travel – life was good.

He started regularly driving across on weekends with some of his sailor friends. Was it normal to drive nearly a thousand miles each way every couple of weeks just to see your girlfriend? Ken always seemed happy, easy-going, generous... but I started to feel vaguely uneasy.

Surviving the Seventies

*

Then my world changed forever. I found out I was pregnant. I waited till Ken arrived the next weekend to tell him. I looked at him as he stood in the doorway of my room, and in an instant I knew I couldn't stay with him forever. But Ken was the first to drop a bombshell. "I'm not going back," he said. He'd deserted from the navy.

I listened as he told me of his decision to leave. Efforts to get a shore posting had failed, and he didn't want to go back to the isolation of Vietnam. He'd told me several times he didn't want me to go to England. "English guys aren't that good," he'd said. I immediately understood the reason he'd deserted was because he feared our relationship would end if he went away.

I went into survival mode. I didn't consider a termination. Abortions were illegal in Australia back then, and after working in the Royal Adelaide Hospital and seeing the results of illegal abortions, I wasn't going down that path. The memory of an Italian girl who'd tried to abort herself with a sliver of wood, contracted tetanus and ended up in an iron lung was enough for me. After an illegal abortion, there was always the chance you wouldn't be able to have more children. I came from a large family and always assumed I'd have kids. I'd been brought up in the Methodist church, and considered terminations murder.

I told Ken we'd have to have the baby adopted as I couldn't tell my conservative family. Ken took the news of my pregnancy calmly. We made plans to go back to Sydney to live when I finished my course in a few months' time. Long-term plans weren't discussed, and I didn't raise the topic.

Ken's easy-going manner changed. He seemed critical of everything – his work, my friends, Adelaide and, in particular, me. Through one of my housemates, he'd got a job working as a labourer on a building site. He hated it after so many years in the navy and resented taking orders from his boss who he detested. He helped himself to a box of fancy taps intended for the house which was nearing completion. "Supplementing the income," he said. I was horrified. I'd never stolen a thing in my life. He had no use for taps, but took them anyway. Eventually he gave them to Hans and Heather in Sydney, for a house they planned to build in Queensland.

I'd just got my driving licence. When we were out driving, Ken would stop the car. "You drive," he'd order, handing me the keys. There was no point refusing. He'd sit in the passenger's seat poised like a cobra, watching my every move.

"What'd you do that for? Stop the car. You're driving like a dick-head."

He'd insist that I drove in the left-hand lane. "But there are always cars parked there," I'd object.

"The road rules are you drive in the left lane unless you're overtaking," he'd order. Ken was hardly one to follow rules, but this gave him the opportunity to yell at me if I didn't weave between the lanes quickly enough. This criticism gave him a perverse pleasure.

He'd picked up a spare battery from somewhere and put it in the boot of the car. I had to run an errand while he was at work and the battery, which I'd totally forgotten about, tipped over and spilled acid all over the bottom of the boot. There was hell to pay when Ken discovered it. He knew I was going out in the car, he knew the battery was in the boot but had also forgotten it. Did he always need someone to blame? Or did he get off on muscle flexing? Often I'd be left a list of things to do while he was at work. The abuse would start if I forgot anything. Even my sewing machine had to be put away and all evidence, such as stray bits of cotton, picked up off the carpet before he got home. I was to give him my undivided attention.

The parking area at our Burwood flat was under the building. Huge pillars supported the storeys above. It was always tricky to park the car, dodging pillars and other vehicles. One evening Ken was in the passenger seat as usual, watching my every move. He yelled at me once too often.

"You park it then," I retaliated. I didn't see it coming. His fist slammed into my face.

"I hate you," I screamed as I ran upstairs to the bathroom to wash the blood from my bleeding nose.

To this day I occasionally feel mildly panicked when driving with a passenger.

The easy-going Ken had been an act; the real Ken was into total control. He'd create a scene in shops if he wasn't served quickly enough, banging on the counter and yelling. I'd stand there wishing the ground would open up. I endured the humiliation of constant criticism in front of his friends. Ken saw me as his possession, bound to him by my pregnancy and financial dependence.

I left two weeks after the baby was born.

Chapter 2

My adoption plans wavered. In the 1960s, most single women who gave birth had their babies adopted. A lot chose to do so – the stigma of being an unmarried mother still stuck firmly. Some were pressured or forced to relinquish their children. A part-Aboriginal woman who I met at CHUMS had a little girl of about four. Her first child, a boy, had been forcibly removed in Papua New Guinea. However, by now it was the early seventies and a lot had changed in a few short years. All the women in the group felt the choice was now theirs. Gough Whitlam's Supporting Mother's Benefit wouldn't be on offer for another year or so, but somehow we managed. My most pressing priority was to get accommodation.

At a CHUMS meeting I met 18-year-old Linda who had a two-year-old, Becky, whose father was in prison. They'd been in a relationship since she was 12. He'd been part of the Darcy Dugan gang, a notorious Sydney bunch of criminals. Darcy had the dubious honour of being New South Wales' most infamous prison escape artist. In 1946 he was being transported by prison tram between Darlinghurst Courthouse and Long Bay Gaol. As the tram passed the Sydney Cricket Ground, he cut a hole in the roof with a kitchen knife and escaped. The tram can be seen today at the Sydney Tramway Museum, presumably with the hole unrepaired... On the wall of the last cell he escaped from he'd written "*Gone to Gowings*".

Linda had run away from home to join her boyfriend in the gang, leaving her frantic family searching for her. Even her detective sergeant stepfather couldn't find her. Eventually, after Becky was born, Linda rang her mother and came back to her family. However, now she was anxious to move out of the home she shared with her mother and stepfather. She and her mother had too many fights. Linda told me that Darcy was a "real nice guy". I got the impression Linda was proud of her association with criminals – it gave her some sort of anti-hero status among her friends.

Linda and I didn't exactly have a huge amount in common; our age difference alone would normally have cancelled each other out as flatmates. However single parents looking for accommodation were thin on the ground and we didn't have the luxury of shopping around. We found a two-bedroomed flat tacked onto the back of an Italian family's home in Ashfield. I didn't want to live in the Inner West. Ken and I had started off living in Burwood in January 1971 when I first came to live in Sydney. Ashfield, the next suburb, was a bit too close to those bad memories. But beggars can't be choosers. Linda had found a government childcare centre for Becky in Redfern, and wanted a place near the railway line.

Linda also got me a job working with her for Telegene, a company with a band of workers who dressed in brown uniforms and cleaned telephones all over the city. But was it effective? Immediately after cleaning, the next user wouldn't catch anything. But what about the following person? And we only cleaned each phone once a fortnight. I considered it a service for companies with more money than sense. Linda and another girl used to while away their time in various Sydney parks instead of cleaning the phones. They were never found out. However, I didn't have to ponder on this too long. After two or three weeks I got a job in a private pathology laboratory in Surry Hills. I'd finished my studies but still had a few months of employment to fulfil the practical side of my traineeship. I would soon have my Diploma of Medical Technology after five long years.

But now it was time to get my baby son back. He'd been in a babies' home in Adelaide for the past two months. I'd gone back to Adelaide two weeks after Danny was born. Ken had reluctantly agreed. I was in a highly anxious state, in a disastrous relationship. My mother and father, oblivious of the fact they were grandparents, had to be told.

Chapter 3

After the dust had settled, I needed time to decide what to do. Going back to Ken was out of the question. I was confident I could bring Danny up myself – after all, I had a brother and sister considerably younger than me, and knew all about caring for babies. But should I? Would he be better off adopted into a two-parent family? Would I be better off free to follow my dreams? I needed time to think. I used what was left of my precious travel savings and went on a package trip to Fiji. Not quite the long boat journey to England I'd dreamed of...

Danny was to be left in the care of the babies' home. The administrator who discussed my situation with my mother and me walked with a limp and was very kind. She said because of the disability she'd been born with, she'd decided not to marry, and had devoted her life to caring for babies in need. I wiped away the tear that was rolling down my cheek. She said that because I was such a nice girl I'd be sure to marry and have more children. What a contrast to the attitude to single mothers in the not so distant past.

*

Fiji was different from anywhere I'd ever been. In my 22 years I'd lived in South Australia and visited New South Wales, the Australian Capital Territory, Victoria and the southern part of Western Australia. This was my first taste of the tropics. I stayed on Castaway Island, off the main island, Viti Levu. There was a handful of people my age and we went water-skiing every day. Water activities were part of the deal and we went out in a glass-bottomed boat to see the coral reefs. Some of us were deposited on a reef to snorkel while the boat took the others further afield. I was paired with an older American guy. We adjusted our goggles and snorkels and swam slowly side by side. The first thing we saw was a shark. I did the proverbial walking on water, but at four-minute-mile speed. This was not my first experience of swimming with sharks.

Surviving the Seventies

When I was a kid in Adelaide, I sometimes went for a swim on summer evenings with our neighbour Mrs Venn when she got home from working in her little milliner's shop opposite Brighton railway station. This particular evening was no different. We walked down the road to the steep path which led to the beach and a few minutes later were wading through the shallows over sand banks and out into water deep enough for swimming. The evening was still and warm, the sea like a mirror. Marino beach is at the end of a long, white sandy beach which stretches away to the north for miles up the coast. To the south lie headlands and rocky beaches. Perhaps because of the abrupt change from sandy beach to rocky headland there are sandbars which extend out to sea. We were a long way from the shore before we reached deep enough water. I loved to swim, and was soon practising my breaststroke.

I heard Mrs Venn yell out, "What's that over there?" She grabbed my shoulder and pointed behind me. I started screaming. About 20 yards away, a large brown fin was cutting through the water straight towards us.

Mrs Venn headed towards the shore, her rotund body ploughing through the water. I was transfixed. I clenched my fists up under my chin and continued screaming. She came to her senses, turned back and grabbed my arm and headed back towards the shore. It felt like we were wading through wet cement.

"Is it still coming? I can't look," gasped Mrs Venn. I looked back. The fin was following us in, still the same distance away, ripples spreading out behind in the calm water in the evening light. The strip of white sand was still way in the distance.

An age passed before we collapsed at the water's edge. Our chests were heaving. When we'd recovered enough to speak, Mrs Venn realised the gold filling in her front tooth was gone. She'd bitten it out in terror. It now lay on the sandy bottom of the sea.

No wonder I had a major panic attack in Fiji. Our salvation, the glass-bottomed boat, was even further away than the sandy Marino beach had been. However, I calmed down when my buddy caught up with me. In reality, it was a very small shark and probably a harmless reef shark. Not like the man-eaters of the South Australian coast where great white sharks like to breed. And to this day I still can't watch *Jaws*.

I don't think I spent my time in Fiji doing much agonised decision-making about whether or not to keep my son. No writing of positive and negative lists. At a very basic level, I felt he was mine. I was the one who had carried him in my body for nine months. And endured the hell of childbirth. Why should I give him away to someone else? He was my son.

*

I'd arrived back in Sydney from Fiji virtually penniless. Before I met Linda and moved to Ashfield, I stayed in the People's Palace, a very large Youth Hostel-cum-backpackers affair, but for people of all ages. Basic but cheap. In no time I was flat broke and didn't eat anything for the two days before my first pay from cleaning telephones. When I got paid I went to the Coles Cafeteria and piled food on my tray. However, two days with no food had dulled my appetite and I reluctantly had to leave most of a sponge slice glistening with red jelly.

Linda came with me to the airport to pick up Danny, who was being flown over in the care of an air-hostess. Ken turned up too, which created yet another anxiety-filled episode. It was my own fault; I should have changed the flight time of the plane and kept Ken in the dark. But I'd been brought up to be responsible for, and feel guilty about, everything. As the elder daughter with three brothers and a sister, it was my role to be my mother's second-in-command. She would never have allotted that role to the males of the family. Back then it was the conservative post-Second World War period and gender roles were well defined. Guilt-ridden at having torn his family apart, I was trying to work something out with Ken. I would never go back to him, but Danny was his son and we both lived in Sydney. Ken could be part of his son's life. Desperate to salvage something of our relationship, Ken paid for the airline ticket for Danny's return.

Linda and I, with Danny in his carry basket, got a taxi home, leaving Ken at the airport. Danny was two months older, chubby and smiling. He'd changed a lot since I'd seen him last. Linda gooed over the baby. She was only 16 when Becky was born but it hadn't put her off babies. I was in a quandary. Ken was Danny's father but my vague plan of Ken being part of Danny's life seemed impossible.

My mind drifted back to that night at Ken's boarding house in North Sydney, the night I'd ended up running for my life in the darkness along Blues Point Road. I'd gone there to talk to him in the hope we could work something out. Our baby would soon be back in Sydney. He had to accept that our relationship as a couple had finished, that we had to figure out where to go from here. It started off pleasantly enough, but suddenly Ken snapped. Perhaps he finally accepted I wasn't coming back. He was in tears. How could I have led him to believe we'd stay together as a family? All the time I was pregnant, how could I have been plotting to leave him?

I was guilt-stricken. Why didn't I defend myself? Had a life of feeling responsible for everything made everything my fault? I had never said I'd stay with Ken. He'd just assumed I would. It had never occurred to him that I could leave.

"You had me in tears every day. Didn't that tell you anything?" I countered in defence.

"I don't know anything about women, I've been in the navy since I was 16," he said.

That at least was true enough.

In an instant, Ken had me pinned to the bed, his hands around my throat. I felt his grip tightening. I was in absolute terror. I looked into his face. It was the face of a stranger. Utterly cold and determined, his dark eyes piercing mine. A vision of my baby son with a murdered mother, and a father in gaol, flashed through my mind. I struggled in desperation, but the soft bed engulfed me. I couldn't push myself up. But once again my guardian angel saved me.

"We'll give it another go, Ken. We'll give it another go."

It was the only thing I could have said to stop him. He released his grip. I sat up, shaking uncontrollably. My hands instinctively rubbed my throat. My mind was racing. I had to get away. The toilet was outside the building, a little away from Ken's room.

"I've got to go to the toilet." As soon as I got outside, I started to run.

When Ken caught up with me in the car and pulled me onto the road, the first thing he said was, "You lied, you bloody bitch."

*

Maybe I was a slow learner, or maybe my years of guilt conditioning addled my reasoning, but I still allowed Ken to see Danny as long as we weren't alone. I finally shut the door on him when Linda and I were still in Ashfield. He'd come around one night to see Danny. Once in my room, he pushed me against the wardrobe and started kissing me. I struggled to get away. Once again he had that expressionless blank look on his face. His eyes fixed on mine, he grasped the lapels of the white lab uniform I was still wearing and ripped it open. The sound of tearing cloth snapped me into action. "Linda," I called feebly. I was back in the grip of terror. By the time she came in, my pantyhose were ripped apart.

Linda was tough. "I'm calling Jack," she said. Jack was her detective-sergeant step-father. Ken, who knew Jack's reputation, left in a hurry. Linda was angry with me for letting Ken come around.

"You're an idiot to let him come here – he's a nutcase," she said savagely.

I could do nothing but apologise. Her parents were worried about Ken being on the scene, concerned about Linda's safety, and more particularly that of little Becky, who they both doted on.

Linda rang her stepfather and the following day Ken was arrested for desertion from the navy, at his job as an electrician at the partly built Opera House.

He served six weeks in the lock-up at Holsworthy Army Base in Sydney's west.

It got him out of my life.

*

I only saw Ken twice more. He came around to work once, to tell me he was married. He and his wife had only known each other six weeks: "This time, I decided to get married before anything happened." Well, he certainly floored me on that one. Firstly, that he'd married someone he barely knew, but most of all that he believed being married would allow him to bully his wife without fear that she'd leave him. He'd thought that my being pregnant meant he owned me. Marriage must have seemed more permanent. He hadn't learned a thing. He then proceeded to tell me that he was still having trouble getting over me! His poor wife.

When Danny was about 18 months old I went to a CHUMS picnic day. Out of the blue, Ken had rung me at work the day before to say he and his wife were moving to the mines of Western Australia and that he wanted to see Danny before he left. I felt ok about it. I figured with so many people around at the picnic, I would be safe enough. Ken had a good camera, all the returned sailors did. They got everything duty-free in Singapore. He took lots of photos of his son.

At one point we walked past the toilets and I needed to go. Ken offered to hold my bag. In a couple of minutes I was back outside and we continued watching Danny as he played with the other kids.

Ken told me his wife had gone home to her mother a few times, but they were still together. I felt sorry for her, but I guess if you marry someone you hardly know, you have to take some responsibility for how things turn out. He also told me that he'd known all along we were living in St Ives, but had decided not to contact me. I knew immediately that he'd opened my bag while I was in the toilet and got my address from my driver's licence. Nothing had changed. I was still the innocent one. And he was still the intimidator.

Years later, when Danny was about six and we were back living in Adelaide, I bumped into Ken's brother-in-law who told us that Ken and his wife were still together, still in WA. I'm afraid I didn't manage to conceal my amazement. Still, I've never been much of an actress. So perhaps my son has siblings somewhere…

That was the last time I heard anything of Ken, and Danny has never showed any interest in finding his father.

Chapter 4

My life in Sydney was hectic. I moved house continually. Linda and I moved to Paddington into a share house with her new boyfriend Phil, her sister and another young guy. I much preferred trendy Paddington to suburban Ashfield. The house was an old terrace above a butcher's shop, right in the middle of Five Ways. The previous tenants had left in a hurry, leaving dusty furniture and dirty dishes sprouting mould. Flies flew in and out of the unscreened windows.

In no time Linda and Phil were in hospital with hepatitis. Linda's mother, understandably upset, was inclined to blame me, saying I should have helped Linda more around the house. I thought this a bit rich. I was working full-time and had a young baby, while Linda and Phil were home all day unemployed, and there were two others living there, one of whom was her sister. Back then, Australian males weren't expected to do any housework. Traditionally when young people left home, rented houses and flats were occupied by the same sex. It was the very beginning of the era of both sexes living together in shared houses and the expectation of dividing household chores was still some time in the future. I stayed home the following weekend and cleaned the house from top to bottom. It took forever. The floors were covered with the latest fashion - thick straw matting which captured all the dirt and filtered it through to the floorboards below.

I'd been thinking of finding somewhere else to live for a while. Linda and I had never had much in common. She wanted to marry Phil, settle down and have more children. I was planning a career and travel. The weekend spent cleaning up after five adults and two children motivated me to start looking.

When I was pregnant I'd read about "The House of Women" in *The Daily Telegraph* newspaper. It was a share house of single women and their children in Wahroonga. *Four Corners* even did a program on them. The fact that it was such a big deal in the media shows how conservative Australian society was at that time. These days it wouldn't make the back page. Even divorce was rare, back then. By coincidence, my friend Heather, who'd come to my rescue on the night I was fleeing Ken, had worked with one of the women. I remembered Leonie from the TV show, and thought she'd come across as somewhat hard. Heather contradicted me: "Oh no, Leonie's really easy-going."

Another coincidence – I was looking through the accommodation section in *The Sydney Morning Herald* and there was an ad for the House of Women. I doubted they would take a baby – all the kids on the TV show were kindergarten age at least. No harm in trying, I decided.

Within a week I was squashed into my new little room in the large sprawling house in Wahroonga. It even had a swimming pool and a housekeeper who looked after the pre-school aged kids so I wouldn't have the drama of child care. Seven women, one guy, and seven kids. Somehow the "no men overnight" rule I'd read about in the paper had fallen aside. Roxanne had moved Leroy, her latest guy, in. Our rent included a wage for the housekeeper, whose role it was to keep the home clean and organise the kids. She took the older ones to school, looked after the younger ones, then did the after-school pick-up. The other women worked. We took it in turns to shop and cook dinner, but otherwise had no household responsibilities. It would have worked well if it weren't for Leroy and Roxanne.

Roxanne was very attractive and smart, but couldn't be alone. She'd had a series of guys since splitting with her husband years before. She had a sad history. She was pregnant when she married, but lost the baby at five months. Her next child, Rachel, lived with us. Her third baby died of pneumonia at six weeks, and her last baby, a girl, went into respiratory distress at birth and only lived a few days. No wonder Roxanne was needy. Leroy was her latest. He was a talented musician and did beautiful leather work, but neither brought in much cash. Roxanne paid the lot. Leroy didn't lift a finger around the house. He happily ate meals paid for by Roxanne and cooked by one of the women. "If there's one thing I won't do, it's dishes," he told me one day as I ploughed through a huge pile, having worked an eight-hour day in the city and cared for Danny when I got home.

Leroy was the consummate leech. I was getting a very different view of males from the gods on pedestals my mother had seen. Roxanne was going through a custody case with her ex-husband, who was understandably worried about the deadbeats Roxanne hung around with. He asked Leonie if she knew Leroy's real name, Leroy Jones being considered more saleable in the music scene than his Spanish birth name. He wanted to find out if Leroy had a police record. I knew his real name, but kept my mouth shut, the Australian culture of not dobbing deeply ingrained.

I was delighted to be living with people I felt in tune with, with the above exceptions. Most Saturdays we preened ourselves and headed off to the Bengal Tiger wine bar in North Sydney. I'd managed to keep my weight down since having Danny, and wore the latest fashions. Since my mid-teens, after being a skinny kid all my life, I'd started putting on weight. Up and down it went. The happiness I felt at being my best weight didn't stop me from putting it back on. I'd always loved food. I'd been cooking my own food when sharing in Ashfield and Paddington and had managed to keep it all under control. Leonie, the workmate of my friend Heather, also struggled with her weight. Our never-ending attempts at dieting cemented our friendship. Predictably, with other people's cooking on offer, back the pounds came. I went from being slim, and in my eyes slim equalled attractive, to squeezing myself into ever-tightening jeans. In no time I was back to my chubby alter-ego. I hated being overweight, as much for the advertising of my lack of self-control as for my appearance.

The underlying motive for these nights at the wine bar was to meet Mr Right, but I felt wary when I met someone new. My former innocent, trusting nature had gone forever, and I subconsciously sized each guy up for potential possessiveness and violence. None of us had much luck. Guys came and went.

Roxanne was a nudist and spent a lot of time wandering naked around the house and sunbathing in the garden. A couple of guys who lived next door spent a lot of time hanging over the fence until they were seen off by Leroy. Barbara was our housekeeper. She was divorced, had a five-year-old daughter and was pregnant following a casual affair in Darwin. She'd decided to have the baby adopted and did the common thing of leaving home so no-one would know. After the baby was born she got her life back on track. Another housemate, Kathy, decided to take over the housekeeper's job, and Barbara went back to work. She started seeing a friend of someone in the house and confided in me, but for some reason her new guy insisted on secrecy and wouldn't let Barbara tell anyone else. We soon found out why – he had his eye on Kathy and soon was openly taking her out. Kathy had no idea of his prior relationship with Barbara. Barbara was very decent about it all and didn't spill the beans. Once again I was flabbergasted about people's heartless behaviour. The past couple of years had been a steep learning curve.

One afternoon we were sitting around the kitchen chatting when someone casually mentioned that her husband had been violent to her. I'd never told anyone about Ken. In my sheltered little world in Adelaide, violence towards women was unheard of. I felt ashamed. It turned out that of the seven women living there, six had been on the receiving end of domestic violence. Once more I was incredulous. Kathy was very casual about the whole thing. Her husband had pursued her down the stairs with a pair of pliers, intent on clipping the diamond off her engagement ring. We all cracked up laughing. Leonie said the fibro panels in the passage of her first home were all broken from her husband throwing her into them. I was a few years younger than everyone else. My education was going forth in leaps and bounds.

I enjoyed living in the house. It made life a lot more straightforward not having to dash off to childcare before and after work. Danny was a happy, placid baby. He slept well and ate well and handled my routine. Even though life was still extremely busy with home, work and socialising, I was happier and more relaxed than I'd been since I found out I was pregnant in September 1970.

But a cloud was appearing on the horizon. Roxanne decided it was Leroy's turn to pay the rent and she stopped paying altogether. "I've paid everything for months," she said to me indignantly. The fact that Leroy had neither an income nor the prospect of getting one didn't seem to enter the equation. Now the five remaining working women were supporting Roxanne, Leroy and Rachel, Roxanne's daughter, as well as the housekeeper, themselves and six children. This went on for several weeks. There were rumblings in the house, but no-one had broached the subject with them. I was furious. I was 22 years old, a single parent, helping to support a family of three as well as myself and Danny.

Eventually Roxanne and Leroy got wind of my complaints and confronted me. I let fly. We had the most unholy row. Leonie and I decided to leave. She'd been on the outer since before I moved in. Personality clashes were inevitable in a household of strong women. I'd been concerned about the swimming pool for a long time. It wasn't fenced and when the phone rang at work I often had this sinking feeling it would be to say that Danny had drowned. Barbara had announced airily once that whenever she couldn't find Danny in the house, she'd first run out and check the pool and then turn on the vacuum cleaner. Danny was intrigued by the sound and would always appear. I was horrified. When I was home and therefore responsible for him, I always knew where he was. Didn't Barbara know it only took two or three minutes for a baby to drown? Another of Kathy's admirers built a play-pen for Danny on the verandah, which made me feel much more relaxed.

*

Angela lived in a new two-storey house in St Ives with her four young children. Her ex-husband had recently left her for Angela's best friend. He was prepared to let his family continue living in the house, but only if Angela rented out rooms to help pay the mortgage and bills. Into this can of worms I moved with Danny, Leonie and her daughter Melanie, and single father Peter with his toddler son.

In no time, Peter and Angela formed a bond. I returned from a few days in Adelaide to be met at the door by the kids, full of news. One night, the ex and his father had entered the upstairs bedroom window via a ladder to take photos of Angela and Peter in bed together. Angela sat up and politely introduced ex-husband and father-in-law to Peter who, being English, went downstairs to make everyone tea. I was shocked by the drama. It all seemed a bit tacky to the part of me which was still the conservative Adelaide girl. And once again, I was presented with the unfathomable thinking of a male who considered it alright to leave his family for a new woman, but couldn't accept a new guy in his ex's life. Or perhaps it was purely mercenary – he stood to gain financially if he could prove adultery on the part of his wife. Apparently the photos were very poor quality.

Leonie and I left. The logistics of the household were far too complex, but it had had its positives. Angela introduced us to the Weight Watchers diet and we all lost about a stone, including Peter who was slim to begin with. She and Peter moved to the North

Coast of NSW, opened an Asian clothing shop, got married and are still there, but with new partners.

*

Our new abode was a sprawling house in Pennant Hills, room enough for four adults plus offspring. Life was still hectic. We roared off to work early each morning, dropping kids at childcare and school en route. I was working in Kensington; Danny was in a childcare centre in North Sydney. Each day was a long struggle through peak-hour traffic. I was often late for work, unavoidable as the centre opened too late to get to work on time.

Very early one morning I headed as usual to the kids' bedroom to wake Danny. There, walking steadily across the green carpet, was a large black and shiny funnel web spider. I yelled for help but the rest of the household slumbered on. I grabbed a glass ashtray off the mantelpiece and dropped it over the creature. We were later told it was a male in search of a mate and that the recent rainy weather had probably driven it inside. Someone transferred it into a glass jar, where it eventually met its end from a blast of insecticide. I would have preferred to hand it to a serum laboratory for venom collection, but arachnophobia won out.

I was still going to CHUMS meetings on occasion. I enjoyed the company of the women I'd got to know and followed their lives with interest. Through CHUMS I met David, a single parent with a son Danny's age. David introduced the household to marijuana, something I'd never come across in Adelaide. I gave it my best shot but, not being a tobacco smoker, didn't have the necessary draw-back skills. David remarked that he hoped it didn't give me a taste for tobacco, which he always mixed with the grass. My aversion to tobacco probably contributed to my failure to perfect the art of marijuana smoking and I reluctantly gave it up.

The share-houses I lived in may have been households of parents and children, but single we were. On Saturdays we preened ourselves for the big night out, just like single people our age everywhere in Australia. I sat around in rollers all afternoon, then teased my hair to make it more voluminous. Flared jeans were in, and we sewed embroidered braid around the cuffs. The weight I'd lost in St Ives crept back on and I forced myself into tight jeans. Leonie had a brand new little yellow car, and off we'd all go heading south to North Sydney and the wine bars. The Bengal Tiger and Stoned Crow were our favourites. We drank a lot of wine and did a lot of talking but no-one ever met Mr Right. The Bengal Tiger delivered me Steve, who I went out with a couple of times. Steve drove a maroon MG sports car, a present from his father for passing his first year in naval architecture. Subtlety wasn't Steve's strong point. When he found out I wasn't on the pill and wouldn't have sex with him, he said he'd come round in a month or so, to give me time to start the contraceptive. I had the feeling Steve's social circle and mine would never overlap.

It was the time of sexual liberation. Women were still coming to grips with their new sexual freedom, while trying to shrug off the double standards of the 1950s and 60s. The Catholics of the households struggled with guilt. I was eternally grateful at having been brought up Methodist. *Cosmopolitan* and *Cleo* were read from cover to cover. An up-and-coming rock star, Ross Ryan, shared our little community. He lived in the cottage alongside our house with his girlfriend. We were seconded into a photography session in the backyard for the album cover of his about-to-be released LP record, *A Poem You Can Keep*. We were given a cassette tape, which we played non-stop for a while. I genuinely liked it. The album was a modest success. Years later, back in Adelaide, I renewed my acquaintance with Ross who was doing the university concert music circuit, and we caught up whenever he was in town. A tenuous link to a time in my life long gone.

*

The relentless grind of peak-hour traffic, rushing to and from childcare, belting into work late and leading a hectic social life took its toll. I lasted six months in Pennant Hills, then moved to Mosman closer to the city. Danny and I shared a three-bedroomed house with Marg, a friend of Leonie's, and her two little girls.

One day at work I got a call from my sister Rosemary who was visiting from Adelaide, to say that Marg was acting very strangely. To make some extra money to supplement her Supporting Mother's Benefit, Marg cared for two young kids after school. She was pressing them to do an art and craft activity, extolling them with "You can do it" when they faltered. Both kids were in tears. When I got home, their mother had collected them and Marg was totally delusional. She thought she was the female version of Jesus Christ come to save the world. Marg's ex-husband Maurice was contacted and her daughters went to live with him.

Marg refused to seek any professional help. Her mother had a mental illness and was doped to the eyeballs. "A pleasant nut" is how Maurice referred to his mother-in-law. Marg was terrified of ending up like her, and you couldn't even say the word "doctor" without her scurrying away. One night Marg woke me about midnight. She'd smoked marijuana and was freaking out. She wanted me to sit up all night with her and talk to her to calm her down. She said she'd pay me for the work day I'd miss. I was out of my depth. My conservative Adelaide upbringing hadn't included counselling. I suggested calling a doctor. At the mere mention of the word she fled from my room and phoned a former lover, Philippe, who came over and sat with her all night. I grabbed a bit more sleep, and staggered off to work.

My grand ambition to travel the world was nearing fruition. I'd committed myself to staying a year in the veterinary laboratory – I felt leaving any earlier would have been poor form. I was earning very good money and living a frugal life. My bank balance expanded.

By now it was several weeks since Marg's breakdown. The lease on the house was nearly up. I was leaving and Marg was in no condition to renew it in her name. I gently prompted her to find another place to live. She'd lost custody of her children. She firmly believed that the colour red represented good, and black, evil. On the day of her custody court case she'd insisted on borrowing my red-and-white checked shirt and even moved the sleeve buttons over to fit her thin wrists. She arrived late at the court as she'd been following a red car, which appeared in front of her as she drove out of Mosman.

When eventually she arrived in court, she decided to plead her own case, Bible in hand. Her solicitors walked out. "Maurice had tears in his eyes," she told me later. I got out scissors, needle and cotton and moved the buttons back.

The day to leave was fast approaching. Thankfully Marg had lined up somewhere else to live and I spent the evenings after work packing. Very late one night I'd had enough and went down the dark passage towards the kitchen to make a cup of tea. Marg came out of her room at the same time, heading towards me up the passage. I screamed when I saw the large butcher's knife in her hand. It was totally innocent – she'd been cutting the string around her boxes of stuff.

It was definitely time to move.

Chapter 5

The mountain tops of Portuguese Timor were pointy and green, with streams tumbling swiftly downwards. I grasped the armrests in the Trans Australian Airlines plane. What a time to develop a flying phobia. Sometimes the planes had to return to Darwin if there was cloud-cover at Baucau airport as there was no radar there. I refused to contemplate that horror.

1974 was one of the wettest monsoons on record. Forty-six years later it still hasn't been surpassed. My planned journey from Adelaide to Darwin had been severely modified.

Back in Pennant Hills, Ross Ryan's girlfriend had told me about the new way of travelling to England via South East Asia, India and Nepal, Pakistan, Afghanistan, Iran and Turkey. The Overland Track.

The Hippie Highway. I was instantly hooked. You were a traveller, not a tourist, and the rules were that you had to avoid flying as much as possible. This was real travel. Planes were too easy, ocean liners passé.

However, the wet season paid no heed to mere mortals. My plans to take the Ghan train from Adelaide to Alice Springs were shelved – the tracks were flooded. I caught the first bus to leave for the Alice in weeks. We stopped in the opal town Coober Pedy late at night and got out for a break. I can still remember a dead mouse on the floor of the underground church. One of my old housemates from Adelaide was now living in Alice Springs and I spent a few days with her, fitting in a bus trip to Ayers Rock. Tourists weren't made aware back then that the rock shouldn't be climbed out of respect for the traditional owners, and I joined a handful of fellow tourists struggling to the safety chain, which was a considerable distance up the steep rock face. Perhaps this separated the sheep from the goats. One of our group, a young English woman, couldn't cope with her fear of heights and had to descend before reaching the security of the fixed chain. She was so disappointed as climbing the Rock had been on the top of her to-do list as she headed back to England. I was overweight and unfit and hadn't done anything so physically hard in years. I jokingly berated the bus driver when we finally got back down, saying he should have warned us and that no-one in their right mind would attempt anything so difficult if they knew what they were in for. He smirked and said he hadn't climbed it himself in years.

One minute it was rain ruining my plans, now it was sand. I'd planned to visit the nearby Olgas but sand across the dirt road made it impossible for vehicles to get there. The only way was a joy flight in a light plane. My fingers dug into the top of the seat in front as the little plane bucked and dived, caught in the hot air columns rising from the hot red rock formations below. An experience, but hardly joyful.

I'd planned to go further north by road from Alice Springs to Darwin, stopping at the Katherine Gorge on the way, but six feet of water over the road at Tennant Creek and the gorge itself being under water saw me flying to Darwin. I was turning into a tourist and hadn't even left Australia. At least we'd touched down in Tennant Creek and Katherine.

I didn't appreciate it at the time, but I was witnessing history in the making through the plane window. There was water as far as the eye could see, roads and fences disappearing beneath the surface, homesteads on islands. Below me was the inland sea that early Australian explorers had sought in vain 150 years earlier. I merely saw it as impeding my grand plan.

We skirted the edge of a cyclone as we made our bumpy descent into Darwin. I caught up with one of the single mothers I'd known in Sydney. She hired a mini moke and we drove around seeing the sights. I'd never experienced such overwhelming heat and humidity, and spent much of my time in Woolworths, which in those far off days was the only place with air-conditioning. I stayed a few days, anxious to leave the familiarity of Australia.

*

The gods smiled on me as we neared Baucau, Portuguese Timor's international airport. Bright sunshine lit up the runway as we touched down.

I was free. Danny was with his grandmother in Adelaide. I'd quit my job. My years of study were over. I gave Danny a big metal fire-engine as a going-away present. It was a large version of his favourite Matchbox toy. "Big one," he said as he opened the box. I told him I was going on a holiday. "Don't take the car," he said. His grandmother's car had obviously struck a chord.

Three years of full-on life in Sydney were behind me. Despite all the dramas, I'd had a good time there. Although I'd often survived on a few hours' sleep and felt worn out, I'd thrived on the fast pace. I didn't look on the Overland Trail as a holiday – this was a serious adventure. I was champing at the bit.

I stayed in the Pearl of the Orient, which didn't live up to its name, but with single rooms at 60 escudos I wasn't complaining. In those days one Australian dollar equalled 38 escudos. South East Asia was looking good. I had chicken for dinner my first night out of Australia. This was long before I read Peter Singer's *Animal Liberation* and became a vegetarian overnight. Scrawny chickens pecked in the backyard. It was indeed a scrawny chicken dinner, more bones than meat. Sixty cents bought an iconically shaped bottle of Mateus Rosé.

A lot of local kids had cleft palates and hare lips, which had not been operated on, far more than you would see in Australia, I thought. But perhaps they stood out because no surgery had been performed. I was told there were only two doctors on the island, but didn't find out whether they attended the locals, or just the colonial Portuguese. The Timorese were tiny, with frizzy hair and dark skin, more Melanesian looking than Asian.

Young Westerners were thick on the ground, some heading south to Darwin at the end of their journey, others like me just beginning, heading deeper into Asia. We were a tribe, brought together by our youth and our common interest in travel. My time in Sydney saving money was a rite of passage. I'd arrived.

The next port-of-call on the Hippie Trail was Dili, the capital of Portuguese Timor. The route from Baucau was my introduction to mountain travel in developing countries – narrow dirt roads with a vertical cliff one side and a precipitous drop the other. I had a fatalistic attitude. These drivers had driven this route countless times. However, I did get out and walk a section when our bus and a truck got jammed together while trying to pass. When they eventually separated and continued, the outside wheels of our bus were partly over the drop. Later, I encouraged one of my South Australian cousins to do the same trip. She spent the entire time in tears of terror, the victim of a driver better suited to the race track, the back of her bus swinging out over the chasm as he hurtled round the bends. Our bus travelled at a leisurely pace, stopping to pick up and deposit locals, pigs, chickens and bags of vegetables. Lunch was chow mein in a little village along the way.

Dili was upmarket with its single set of traffic lights. I headed for the Hippie Hilton, a tin shed on the beach where travellers on the cheap unrolled their sleeping bags on the cement floor. I loved the clothes the recent arrivals from Indonesia and India were wearing. Loose, flowing and colourful, made of cotton or rayon. Becoming a hippie was going to suit me right down to the ground. I was trying to lose weight and these were flattering fashions. I surreptitiously packaged up my hair dryer and sent it back to Adelaide. Only tourists carried hair dryers. I wasn't going to let my fellow travellers find out what a novice they had in their midst. Wild hair was the go. Oh the relief of not trying to tame my unruly hair... this was heaven.

Cock fighting was a Timorese passion, like horse-racing in Australia. This was the real Timor, I thought, and took myself along to an afternoon session. A lot of money changed hands. A Chinese man had champion birds which slashed viciously into their opponents at lightning speed. Every time his bird won he held it aloft in both hands and did a victory dance around the ring, while the owner of the loser quietly rung its neck in the corner, if it wasn't already dead. I left in disgust after a few rounds.

Bored and lonely young Portuguese soldiers wandered the streets. They were called up for four years, and spent much of that time in Portugal's colonies of Timor, Mozambique, Angola or Guinea Bissau. Marriages between the soldiers and locals were common, but they weren't allowed to fraternise with the travellers, to their mutual disappointment.

The markets in Dili were the place to shop for travellers on a tight budget. I was walking back to the beach bearing peanuts, bananas and a coconut when I was approached by a young Timorese guy on a motorbike. He had written an article in English for *The Australian* newspaper, and wanted a native speaker to check it. He introduced himself as Jose Ramos Horta, editor of the Dili newspaper. We went to his mother's house, some distance out of town, a wooden place on a lot of land. I suspected they were well off by local standards.

I read the article, the contents of which I've now forgotten. The English was near perfect. It never occurred to me to wonder how a young guy of my own age, 24 years, brought up on an impoverished island under Portuguese colonisation for 400 years, could write such perfect English. Jose's father was Portuguese, his mother Timorese. He had numerous brothers and sisters. He'd spent some time in Mozambique, banished by the Portuguese because of his political activities.

I saw a lot of Jose during my time in Dili, riding everywhere on the back of his motorbike. This motorbike was popular with Jose's little nephew Georges, who was three years old. Every morning he would ride with Jose to the newspaper office, stay a little while, and then Jose would take him back home. I have thought of little Georges from time to time, and wondered if he survived the future Indonesian occupation, unlike several others in Jose's family.

One afternoon we were sitting on his verandah. Jose ordered one of his sisters who was passing to bring us coffee. His tone was abrupt. The feminist in me baulked at this example of gender inequality. Women's Liberation was a long way down the list of priorities in colonial Portuguese Timor. Jose had also invited a young Dutch guy who was en route to

Darwin and staying in the Hippie Hilton. He lowered his six feet plus frame into a deckchair on the verandah. The canvas held out momentarily then split, depositing him onto the floorboards. Most Timorese were half his weight.

The Dutchman had suspended his food bag from a beam above his sleeping area in our accommodation, as protection from the rats, mice and insects, which were quite at home there. The following morning he showed me his cheese, with neat grooves all the way down one side. "Ants," he announced confidently. I peered closely. More likely a rat's front teeth, I thought, but kept my mouth shut.

A young English guy also heading for Darwin came home late one night and could be heard throwing up noisily in the toilet cubicle in the corner. The retching was soon followed by several sharp screams. The next morning, he told me he'd been shut in with a rat, which ran round and round to their mutual terror.

I set out to buy a ticket for the midnight barge from Dili to Batugade near the Indonesian border. I was devastated to find all the tickets had already been sold. All my new friends were going on that barge. I ran to Jose's office to see what strings he could pull. He tried to persuade me not to catch the barge but to fly instead. He'd taken the barge once himself and said it was very crowded and a buffalo had given birth. This only served to inspire me more. What could be better than sailing overnight under tropical stars in a vessel packed with Timorese, Western travellers, cargo and animals? He eventually relented and one phone call later my passage was assured.

I said goodbye to Jose and joined my fellow travellers on the barge, never dreaming for one second that I had been in the company of a future Nobel Peace Prize winner.

A few weeks later there was a coup in Lisbon and the Portuguese deserted the island. After 400 years there was minimal infrastructure. They left the former colony impoverished and in a political vacuum, taking with them the two doctors who treated the entire population.

I followed East Timor's misfortunes over the years. I was in India at the end of that year when I got a letter from my mother telling me of the deaths of the Australian television crews on the border with Indonesian Timor, saying she was very sad for our neighbours, the Venns. Mrs Venn was my swimming companion in the shark episode on Marino beach. Their daughter Shirley was married to Greg Shackleton, one of the Channel 7 reporters, and I'd gone to their wedding as a teenager in Adelaide. Balibo, where they were killed, is near Batugade, our destination on the Dili barge.

Occasionally I got news of Jose via newspapers and television. He was living in New York, promoting the cause of East Timor and even addressed the United Nations. He came to Adelaide on a speaking tour in the 1980s, trying to rally support from our pro-Indonesian government. I was a member of the Campaign for Independent East Timor and went up to him after his talk. I reminded him of the carefree time we'd had in the former Portuguese Timor, riding around on his little motorbike.

He stared at me. "You look different," he said, puzzled. "I've lost some weight since then," I answered, feeling virtuous that I'd now managed to keep my weight down for several years. I politely refrained from pointing out that he'd put weight on.

I hugged him goodbye, a tireless worker for a cause given up as lost by the world.

I can still remember a political cartoon from the Adelaide *Advertiser*. It showed a map of Australia with East Timor to the north in flames. "*Shame Australia Shame*" read the caption. Years later, I watched Jose on TV as he descended the plane steps on his return to East Timor following their independence from Indonesia. The expression on his face could only be described as beatific. He went on to serve as both Prime Minister and President of the newly independent Timor Leste.

Later still I watched more footage as Jose was evacuated to Darwin, near death with a bullet in his chest from an assassination attempt, another victim of the endless internal fighting between opposing Timorese political factions. He eventually returned to political life, but has now retired to live a quieter life in his beloved homeland.

*

My trip on the barge was uneventful compared to Jose's episode with the buffalo. We lounged on the deck, propped up against our rucksacks, squashed between cargo and passengers, and managed to sleep on and off. The night was calm and no city lights dimmed the brightness of the stars. Just one minor drama – my bottle of face cleanser leaked all over my tampons, which proved very difficult to replace in the outer reaches of the Indonesian empire.

We arrived at our destination early the next morning. Batugade was a quiet little village, on the Portuguese side of the border with Indonesian West Timor, not far from Balibo, which would attain notoriety the next year as the site of the murder of the Australian TV journalists by the invading Indonesian army.

We sat around most of the day waiting for a truck, the local transport from Batugade across the border to Atapupu in Indonesian Timor, 16 kilometres away. In those days that seemed to me an impossibly long trek carrying a rucksack. At about three o'clock boredom overcame us and nine from the waiting group set out to walk to the border post and a new country. The road was still a quagmire from the wet season. I joined two New Zealanders, Jan and Marilyn, who were as slow and unfit as I was. At one spot we got bogged in the mud up to our knees and laughed so much we had to drag ourselves out and run into the bushes before we wet ourselves. An American woman in her fifties was really travelling light. All her worldly goods were in two local woven baskets, one slung over each shoulder. In one particularly muddy patch disaster struck. The handle on one basket snapped, upending all her gear in the mud. The American gazed down at the lotions and potions disappearing into the ooze. "I don't need any of that junk," she said, and continued on her way.

Document checking was a serious affair. Our passports were first examined at a little post right on the border itself. Later, when we finally arrived in Atapupu having been picked up at last by a local bus, we had to leave our papers at the police station overnight. We found a little café selling nasi goreng, had dinner, then slept on the beach, our first night in Indonesia. I hadn't realised how hard sand is to sleep on.

Our deliverance from Atapupu came in the form of the Golden Wheel, a bus of sorts, which laboured between the border and Kupang, the capital of

Indonesian Timor. A bit further along the road at the town of Atambua we had our passports stamped and finally set off for Kupang.

The Golden Wheel was the trip of a lifetime, though not in the conventional sense. In all my years of travel, nothing has come near it. The wooden bench seats were not designed for large Westerners. Latecomers and their bags were sardined into the aisle. After half an hour we turned back – the driver had forgotten a passenger who'd already paid his fare. By the time we got going again it was four o'clock.

As we stopped and started, picking up passengers along the way, a young guy with wild curly hair and wearing blue denim bib and brace overalls caught my eye. Charley was practising his Bahasa with the locals.

"How are you?" they'd call in English through the windows as we passed.

"Baik baik saja," Charley yelled loudly and often, straight from the guide book. However, the old Dutch "j" still lingered in many publications, the correct pronunciation being *saya*. Charley's laughter and enthusiasm were infectious and I felt instantly drawn to him.

The wet season was not the season to be travelling this road, let alone in the worst wet season in decades. An hour down the track we got bogged. The bus was jammed in mud up to the bottom of the door. The crew dug as showers fell. A rope was attached and everyone pitched in, pulling on the rope or pushing from behind. Six hours later we were on our way, crammed wet and muddy back on the benches.

Salvation lasted a full 10 minutes. A rifle shot jolted us from our torpor. A tyre had blown out. The bus had a spare tyre and tube but no wheel. It took two hours to manhandle the old tyre off and the new one on. At least it gave us a chance to stretch our cramped bodies while we waited. We had just got going again when there in middle of the road in front was an utterly bogged truck. Our driver and crew, defeated at last, settled down for what remained of the night. Inside the bus, it was beyond uncomfortable. After a while, Jan the New Zealander and I extracted ourselves as dawn approached and lay down on the roadside on my plastic cape. It seemed the better option. Of course this decision coincided with the freeing of the bogged truck and we dragged ourselves back on board the Golden Wheel.

Notes from my diary:

> I can't remember how many times we got bogged in the muddy roads. It became a matter of course to get out and pull and push. The Indonesian driver and his crew were terrific – working all night in the mud and slush.

We were a well-oiled team. No-one complained; the situation was so ludicrous that laughter broke out every time we got bogged yet again.

Kupang and salvation lay ahead. The countryside became drier the further west we travelled and consequently the roads improved. We could taste victory. But the gods weren't smiling on this journey – about 50 kilometres from the capital a washed-away bridge finally defeated the Golden Wheel. Tiny Timorese men held our arms as we waded across the shallow but fast-rushing river. We rewarded them with a few coins and slumped on the far bank, resigned to another long wait for transport. Six hours later deliverance came in the form of an open-topped truck. We arrived in Kupang at midnight, 24 hours behind schedule.

I wrote in my diary:

> Kupang has a lot of character with winding narrow roads and many hills. The streets are full of potholes and very slushy after rain, and have open sewers. The buildings are old and very tightly crowded together. There are countless little shops and street stalls. Must comment on the toilets and bathrooms here. The toilets are just a hole in the ground with two places for the feet. No toilet paper – just a dipper full of water. You're meant to use your left hand. The "bath" or "shower" is a big square tub of

water and you stand next to it and pour the water over yourself. No soap in the tub.

I was delighted – this was the real Asia.

But the real Asia had its drawbacks. Several of our group were suffering from the effects of different approaches to hygiene in the first and third worlds. We drank tea in a local café and thought up titles for our book: *Through Asia on the Run* and *Across Asia on the Trot*, by Will E. Makit. I took a photo of buildings hanging over the sea, their foundations eroded by centuries of tides.

Cargo ships plied their trade amongst the islands between Timor and Java to the west: Flores, Sumba, Sumbawa, Komodo, Sangeang, Lombok, Bali... this was the stuff of romance, the Far East of early European explorers. Of course one could fly, but real travellers went by sea. I hoped to catch a ship which stopped at all the islands.

When I was in primary school in Seacliff, an outer Adelaide suburb, my teacher took us to the very first Adelaide Festival of Arts. We were to see David Attenborough, a British naturalist. I'd always been interested in nature study, as the subject was then called, and was enthralled. It's hard to reconcile the young Attenborough, then in his twenties, with the now 94 year-old still following his dreams. I remember his enthusiasm in 1960, much the same as he is today. What grabbed my interest were the Komodo Dragons; I'd always been interested in lizards and had kept several as pets. In Kupang, when I discovered that Komodo lay between Timor and Java I was determined to go there. At last I would see these mythical creatures in the flesh.

But alas, it was not to be. These cargo ships travelled irregularly, some island-hopping, others sailing directly to Java. Ours was a direct route. Waiting for the next ship wasn't an option – it could be weeks away. Sadly, I shelved that particular dream. Not so an English guy who decided to sit it out in Kupang. My last memory of him is of watching him soak his sleeping bag in a bucket of water, having used it as a tablecloth while cutting up papaya.

My first impression of our ship, the *Pulau Sangeang*, was that it was very large and very rusty. I joined six of the Golden Wheel survivors together with one newcomer and boarded the *Sangeang* early in the afternoon. One of my shipmates was Jud, a former schoolmate at my old primary school. Not however in my class which went to see David Attenborough. We settled ourselves on the deck of the bow in the open air, by now inured to waiting. We cast off at 10 o'clock, on a dead-calm sea on a very black night, and headed west into the Sawu Sea.

Below decks sweltered a teeming throng of Chinese and Indonesians. I checked out the toilets, all down below. One look was enough. I took two Lomotil tablets, designed to stop the movements of the lower intestine, intended for diarrhoea on bus trips. Marilyn, the other New Zealander, came up with a solution. Envious that the males could easily relieve themselves overboard and not face the toilets, she'd perched her behind over the rails. After darkness fell I found myself a private spot, rearranged my clothing and eased myself onto the rail. I hadn't factored in the height of the rail – my feet were off the deck. I was teetering above the ocean in the middle of the Flores Seas. One wrong move and I would be treading water in the blackness, the ship steaming off into the distance. Horrified, I lurched forward onto the deck. It was the tail-end of the era of sea voyages between Europe and Australia and people sometimes did disappear, obviously gone overboard. I occasionally still have horrors thinking of struggling to keep afloat through the night watching the distant stern of the ship. My guardian angel was still with me. She must have classified me as a hopeless cause by now.

Food was included in the fare and we had two meals a day, one at ten in the morning, the other at 5.30 pm, consisting of boiled rice, a few boiled green vegetables and one piece of nearly inedible dried fish, usually the head. Perhaps my plan to lose a few kilos would be realised.

After being out of sight of land for most of the day, the island of Flores loomed on the horizon, part of a spine of volcanoes which runs through the archipelago. Several perfect classic peaks touched the clouds, silhouetted against the blue sky.

Jud was a bit of a wag and taught us the old sailors song, *Friggin' in the Riggin'*. I still sing the chorus – "*because there was f'... all else to do*" – if I'm idle. He had a repertoire of jokes, which helped while away the hours. Everyone carried a book to read and swap with other travellers. I had a copy of *Across Asia on the Cheap,* the very first Lonely Planet guidebook. In those days it was a thin little paperback, its cover black and white. It detailed the Overland Trail, starting in Australia, then proceeding through Portuguese Timor, Indonesia, Singapore, Malaysia, Thailand, Indo-China, Burma, India, Nepal, Pakistan, Afghanistan, Iran, Turkey and finally into Europe via Greece. How to find cheap accommodation, when to travel, where to eat cheaply, what to see and, most importantly, what to pay. A lot has happened since Tony and Maureen Wheeler put the little book together on the kitchen table of their flat in Melbourne in 1973. Lonely Planet fetched $244 million when sold in 2011, and it's no longer possible to travel through some of the Middle Eastern countries described in that modest first publication.

I awoke at dawn the next day as we sailed between Sumbawa and the elusive Komodo. So near, and yet a world away. By now much of our conversation centred around what we were going to eat when we reached Surabaya, our destination on eastern Java. Rice and fish heads were beginning to pall.

A broken water pump marked our fourth day on board. It was Good Friday, and we were told there would be no more fresh water until Java. I shook my half-full water bottle nervously but they managed to fix the pump later in the day. At last we seemed to have left the wet season behind. Sea breezes kept the tropical heat at bay during the day, the nights were still and cool. Lombok appeared, its volcanic peaks obscured by clouds. Dolphins swam in the bow wake, the water dead calm. We hung over the rails to watch them, the ship perfectly mirrored in the sea below. Flying fish, their fins spread like wings, accompanied us, skimming the surface for metres before disappearing. In the evening the lights of Bali appeared on the horizon to the south. We gazed wistfully at our true destination. Bali was the place to be on the Hippie Highway, a Hindu gem of magic mushrooms and marijuana, emerald rice paddies and perfect waves.

Chapter 6

Very early the next day we woke to see Java off the port side and Madura Island to starboard. Five days and four nights on the *Sangeang* had cured me of sea voyages for the moment. Our destination, the seductively named Surabaya, was calling...

Sadly, Surabaya's name was the only seductive thing about it – Indonesia's second largest city was crowded, polluted, noisy and dirty. We got a bus to the Transito Inn Youth Hostel where a dormitory bed cost 100 rupiah, a pittance. A wash never felt so good. One of our group, Don, broke the rules and jumped fully clothed into the cement tub filled with water instead of ladling it over himself. He squelched through the dining room, water running out of his sandshoes. We laughed, but the staff probably rolled their eyes at these Western barbarians.

We all went out for tea and had chop suey, coke, wine and beer which was great after the garbage on the boat. Jan, Marilyn and I went for a tour of the city. It's an incredible place. There are cars, motor scooters, betjaks (scooter taxis) and bikes roaring through the streets at an incredible pace. Lord knows what their accident statistics are. We had several cakes from roadside stalls en route. There are many big department stores selling every possible thing and we were plagued by little Indonesians trying to sell us wood carvings etc. Saw several beggars, usually crippled, sitting on the footpaths.

Went to the fruit market and the largest general market. They have literally hundreds of stalls crammed together with tiny little alleyways between them (usually very muddy). I tried a tropical fruit, a salak, I'd never seen before and Jan and I bought a beautiful big pawpaw or "papaya" as they're called here. It had pink flesh instead of the usual orange.

One of our group, an Australian girl, went off exploring alone. When it was time to come back to our hostel, she realised she hadn't taken note of either the name or address. We'd all piled into betjaks at the port and let Don who'd been to Surabaya before instruct the drivers. She finally collapsed into the communal lounge area at 11 pm, after being driven fruitlessly all around the city and eventually finding a driver who recognised "youth hostel". A trick for young players, I thought, and made a mental note to always remember both the name of accommodation and the address in future.

A couple of days in this chaos were enough, and we caught the bus back east to Bali. Luxury at last. Our transport was a modern bus, which even had reclining seats and a free supper. I fell asleep immediately. A ferry transported us, bus and all, across the Selat Bali, the Bali Straights, a narrow passage between the two islands. We continued through the night and arrived in the capital, Denpasar, early the next morning. We stepped into a world of Hindu statues, shrines and little offerings of flowers on banana leaves – what a contrast with Surabaya.

Kuta Beach was the in-place for real travellers. I was soon there, settled in the little Losmen Radiasa, simple family-owned accommodation, sharing a room with a Canadian girl I met there. No-one stayed alone in a double room by choice. Watching every cent was part of the scene.

The Radiasa had a central courtyard filled with tropical plants and flowers. Our rooms bordered this courtyard, each opening on to a verandah with cane tables and chairs. Every morning we were greeted by family members bearing smiles, tea and bananas.

Their names created great confusion. There are only four Balinese names, depending on your order of birth in the family. First born is Wayan, followed by Made, Nyoman and Ketut. If there are more than four children, which is usually the case, you just start with Wayan all over again. I asked how massive confusion is avoided in the wider community when trying to identify people, as no-one seemed to have a surname. Apparently identification is linked to your local temple. However I noticed that a lot of younger Balinese called themselves by another name, often Western. A sign of things to come.

A month had now passed since I'd left Adelaide. My restlessness to keep on the move was fading, mostly due to the influence of my fellow travellers who were nearly all just-graduated university students. They really knew how to relax. I'd come from a background of full-time work, single parenthood, and fairly serious partying. I was used to firing on all cylinders. Life in Kuta soon became a mixture of swimming in the surf, lying on the sand and eating at the dozens of little restaurants. A favourite was Mama's, which served a huge vegetarian smorgasbord every night for a pittance. The table was a work of art – traditional vegetable dishes, fruit salads, banana custard and banana fritters. Another place, the Baliyos, made fruit drinks of banana and pawpaw so thick you had to eat them with a spoon. I had hoped to lose weight with all the hard travelling and walking around new places in the tropical heat. It wasn't happening.

Jan and Marilyn, the New Zealanders, were used to leading a decadent student's life. They dragged me along to the Garden Restaurant, which served magic mushroom omelettes. The magic came from the hallucinogenic blue meanie mushrooms which adorned the omelette's surface. We spent the whole afternoon laughing; everything struck us as hysterical. The active ingredient, psilocybin, must stimulate the pleasure centre of the brain. That evening as we recovered on the beach the sunset was truly memorable. The clouds lifted to reveal a line of perfect volcanic peaks silhouetted against pink sky.

A Kuta tradition was to sit on the beach every evening, smoking marijuana and watching the sunset. My attempts at dope smoking had been put on hold in Sydney as I couldn't stomach the tobacco invariably mixed with it. However, in Bali the dope was so cheap no-one bothered to mix it and I succumbed to peer pressure to take it up again. After a drug-enhanced sunset everyone wandered back into the village as darkness fell, to have dinner. Jan, Marilyn and I, overcome with anticipation of our next culinary delight, rarely stayed until dark. We referred to our hasty departure as the Gourmet's Gallop. Our appreciation of the food far outweighed that of the scenery. No doubt marijuana-induced hunger, known as the munchies, contributed.

Jan and I made the acquaintance of a Javanese artist, Soerono, and visited his studio.

> He's a fascinating little guy, about 60, very tiny with long grey hair to his shoulders. He paints, makes sculptures and does batik. He made us more than welcome, got us coffee then showed us how to make batik. He used lengths of white poplin stapled to a frame to keep it taut and drew the outline of his design with blue crayon. He then painted over the outline with a special elastic wax using pipe-shaped instruments with tubes of varying dimensions coming out of the base.
>
> The wax is put in the bowl of the pipe and runs out the tube. The background is done with a more brittle wax painted on with flat paint brushes. This produces the "crackling" effect when dyed. Soerono mixed several bowls of dye and salts, and dyed two batiks using the same set of dyes. One was in browns and yellows, the other in reds, mauves and blues. They are as brilliant as a stained glass window when held up to the light. Some dyes he applied with brushes, others by immersing the whole print.
>
> He asked if he could paint our portraits the next day in return for letting us make a small

piece of batik. Of course we agreed. We had lunch with him and left at two pm, after being there five hours absolutely fascinated. Had my portrait painted in oils, and it only took one and a half hours. He was all keen on painting me nude but I wangled out of that one. Had to keep my distance all evening as he's very "handy".

A sad story came out later as we worked on our batiks. "Last month thief come," Soerono told us. "All batiks gone. Studio full of batiks to sell." He waved his hand towards the back of the room. "Nearly 50 finished batiks, all gone. It's Javanese. They come here now because of tourists." A Javanese himself, Soerono blamed Javanese youths drawn to Bali by the attractions of Western culture created by tourism.

I still have my two little batiks, one a Taurus bull, my birth-sign, the other an octopus in oranges, reds and yellows.

My Canadian roommate asked if I wanted to see classic Balinese dances. I asked my New Zealand friends to come with us but they were planning yet another night of raging. We saw five dances based on stories from the Hindu Ramayana. The dancers were tiny, slim Balinese girls, clothed in gorgeous costumes, their black hair pulled back tightly, their faces heavily made-up. They were accompanied by an all-male Gamelan orchestra of xylophone-like instruments, drums, flutes and gongs.

Religious ceremonies and dancing are woven through Balinese day-to-day life. An open-air theatre shared the side fence with our losmen. My roommate moved on, her time in Bali coloured by the theft of her favourite jeans, which had disappeared off the washing line at the losmen. Her place was taken by Charley, the Golden Wheel veteran with the wild curly hair and bad Bahasa. I was secretly pleased as there was something appealing about Charley's open friendliness. He fitted the hippie stereotype – afro hair, denim overalls, fondness for marijuana, university-educated...

We hung over the fence when darkness fell and watched the Barong and Kris dances next door. Male dancers worked themselves into a trance and stabbed at their bodies with daggers (kris), but the skin was never broken. Some were carried off, seemingly unconscious.

Ulu Watu temple perches on top of a sheer cliff dropping 90 metres straight down into the Indian Ocean and legend has it that the temple is a ship turned to stone. The surf below sometimes reaches eight metres in height and is considered the island's biggest challenge by the surfing fraternity. Marilyn and I tore ourselves away from Kuta and hitched south to the temple, by way of a car and two trucks. Way below, hundreds of tuna had stranded themselves on the beach and the villagers were carting them off by the truck load.

A family of monkeys lived among the shrines and statues. I fed them biscuits but the large dominant male took the lot. When I by-passed him and handed a biscuit to one of the females, he flew at me, mouth open, his long canine teeth bared. I quickly gave him the packet and developed a healthy respect for monkeys.

Our journey back to Kuta was very smelly, perched on top of a pile of fish in the back of an open truck.

After a week or so of the good life, the New Zealand contingent and I caught a bus to the mountains. Our lives were becoming too comfortable. I felt it would be embarrassing to confess that all I'd seen of Bali was Kuta Beach. Our destination, Mt Batur, lay on the opposite side of the island. We meandered our way amid villages linking the southern and northern shores. Although the journey only took three hours, a lunch stop was on the schedule. By now I'd just about become acclimatised to the leisurely pace of the tropics.

Kintamani village on the slopes of Mt Batur was our home for the night. The houses were drab and dirty from volcanic ash, becoming even more sombre as fog and mist descended in the late afternoon. A small pack of dogs followed us as we wandered. Lean, scarred and mangey, they were typical of many dogs to be seen throughout Indonesia. A couple started to bark at us in a half-hearted way. Jan turned and barked over her shoulder, whereupon the dogs became emboldened and rushed to within inches of our heels. Marilyn and I hissed at Jan under our breath as we quickened our pace up the road with a now loudly barking pack at our ankles. I added dogs to my list of Balinese animals to be treated with respect.

The setting for Kintamani's Hindu temple just about rivalled that of Ulu Watu's. Built right on the edge of the valley, it overlooked the active volcano Gunung Batur. At night when the mist lifted the volcano was a black silhouette against the sky with streams of glowing lava flowing down its side. Every few minutes a great shower of lava and rocks was thrown into the air with a rumbling which sounded like a plane.

Earlier that morning, we'd been told about a Pan Am jet en route from Hong Kong to Denpasar which had crashed in the mountains near Puloki in Bali's north west, killing all 107 people on board. Back in Kuta a few days later, we were accosted by entrepreneurial Balinese touting for passengers for their tours to the crash site. I politely declined. I was going through a fear-of-flying stage and didn't need to compound the problem.

I was keen to climb the nearby volcano but couldn't motivate the New Zealanders. Perhaps volcanoes weren't a novelty to them. They accompanied me to Penelokan village on the shores of Lake Batur beneath the mountain where we parted company.

I joined up with Clive, a young Canadian, and together we hired a guide to take us to the top. The slope was very steep, the weather hot and humid. I was unfit, overdressed except for my footwear (thongs), and without food or water. Before long I was in a sauna. I took off my jeans, tugged at my T-shirt which fortunately was long, until it more or less covered my chubby thighs, and struggled after the others. The Canadian was an old hand who had been working in Indonesia for some time. He gave me a bottle of soft drink and an orange, and went on and on about his wife who'd left him for another man. I made sympathetic noises. A small price to pay, I figured, for salvation from dehydration.

We sat on the volcano's edge overlooking the active crater and ate our oranges. Huge billows of smoke were blown out continually. Every few minutes a great spurt of rock and ash blasted into the air, accompanied by very loud rumblings. One of my thongs had broken on the way up and I burnt my foot on hot ash which had fallen onto the ground.

On the surface it looked like whitish dust, but underneath were glowing embers.

I'd landed on my feet bumping into Clive. He had the day all planned out. Next on his itinerary were hot springs on the edge of Lake Batur. We began our descent from the crater and after a few kilometres arrived at the springs. They were only about nine inches deep, but felt wonderful on my aching muscles. I lolled on my back and surveyed the lake through half-closed eyes. However, indolence wasn't on Clive's agenda and I was soon drip-drying as we chugged across the water in an old wooden boat with an outboard motor. Our destination was Trunjan village, home of the Bali Aga, the oldest inhabitants of the island. We couldn't enter the temple as a villager had died the previous day and no-one is allowed to enter for three days following a death.

Further around the lake was the cemetery where bleached skulls and bones were scattered over the ground. Several skulls were neatly lined up along a little wall, their fixed grins unsettling. Our guide blamed Javanese sightseers for this act of irreverence. The body of a middle-aged woman lay on her back in a very shallow open grave covered with a tent-shaped structure fashioned out of widely spaced bamboo slats. She was fully dressed in a bright sarong, blouse and head scarf. Only her face was exposed. Flies crawled in and out of her parted lips. Bodies of the

Bali Aga are left to decay naturally in the open air, until just the bones remain. I've since learned that the Bali Aga of Trunjan no longer use this cemetery and now have a new and secret location. Another sign of the times.

Back in Kuta Beach I was secretly delighted to find Charley was still there in our room at the Losmen Radiasa, and no-one had joined him. I moved back in. We drifted into wandering around together, lying on the beach, eating, smoking dope. We had so much to talk about, our passion for this big trip of a lifetime, our lives in Australia, our previous relationships. The relaxed lifestyle, free from the normal hassles of everyday living back home, made friendships so easy here. One night we were back in our room, reading in our separate single beds. "You can hop in here with me if you like," Charley said, in his usual relaxed manner.

I must have taken a bit long to reply. He laughed. "You don't have to, you know."

I was more reserved than Charley, but was soon out of my narrow bed and sharing his.

Chapter 7

The afternoon of my 25th birthday was spent on board the *Tampomas* languishing in port in Jakarta. If one overlooked the toilets, this was an upmarket vessel compared with the *Sangeang* which took us between West Timor and Java. I'd left Charley behind in Bali. His pace was more laidback than mine. Nevertheless we'd been bumping into each other at the various travellers hang-outs between Bali and Jakarta, and as luck would have it he'd arrived in Jakarta the previous night. Even better, he was booked on the same boat. Our destination was Tanjungpinang, a little island just off Singapore.

Predictably, we left port at midnight, heading north between Sumatra and Borneo into the black tropical night. Eventually rain drove us off the deck and we slept in the first-class corridors. No-one seemed too concerned but we were asked to leave at dawn. I felt off-colour all day but couldn't blame seasickness as the sea was the usual mill-pond.

Transport to Tanjunpinang was via a long boat as the *Tampomas* had anchored off-shore. It was overfilled with people and cargo, and the Westerners had a very long and loud argument with the skipper as he was charging the natives 50 rupiah and us 200 rupiah. He cut the motor several times but eventually took us to the wharves.

Travelling on the cheap involved being ever-vigilant against rip-offs. Even scruffy hippies were seen as a bottomless well of wealth, which we were in comparison with the locals. I had saved a lot of money working at Sykes and Partners, the veterinary laboratory in Kensington, during my last 12 months in Sydney, but not all my fellow-travellers were so well-heeled. Taking up to a year to travel between Australia and Britain was common, and watching every cent became second nature. I still smile when I picture an Australian couple on a very tight budget, telling off one of our group for paying too much for a freshly laid egg. "You're inflating the market," they complained.

Charley had a particular motivation for visiting Singapore – he'd been born there. His father had been in the British Navy and was stationed there for two years. We were concerned that Charley's wild curly hair would be cut off when we went through customs. Singapore kept a strict eye on its youth and didn't want them corrupted by the evil west. Compulsory haircuts were common. However the customs clerk on seeing *Country of Birth: Singapore* in Charley's passport, struck up a friendly conversation and waved us through. Some unfortunates had "Suspected Hippie" marked in their passport, and were shunted quickly to Malaysia.

We found the old bungalow, by now deserted and overgrown with tropical foliage, where Charley had lived as a baby. I was surprised it was unoccupied. It was a large and sturdy house with a big yard, and housing must have been at a premium on such a small island. I have a photo of Charley on the verandah at the top of the steps, smiling broadly.

Although he'd escaped the barber's shears, after a few days Charley had his hair cut. Perhaps the humidity was getting to him. I'd loved his trendy afro, and took quite a while to get used to his new clean-cut look.

We did the usual touristy things – visited Change Alley with its little shops all crammed together, selling everything from chopsticks to cheongsams. We had dinner at the huge Orchard Road carpark open-air night market, noodles cooked on the spot at one of the countless little stalls, followed by big pieces of pineapple. At midnight we were in Bugis Street for the transvestites' spectacular, but to sit and relax and take in the experience required the purchase of an extortionately priced drink. I'd seen Les Girls in Kings Cross in Sydney, starring the famous Carlotta, but as a distant member of the audience. Now close up, I was intrigued by these flamboyant characters who sashayed amongst the servicemen, middle-aged tourists and young travellers, causing blushes and giggles by sitting on the occasional knee. They had very big hair and were heavily made-up, especially around the eyes.

One bizarre experience followed the other:

We went out to the Tiger Balm gardens. What an incredible place! There's no continuity in their set up – they'll have a scene of plaster figures representing some ancient Chinese torture with nothing left to the imagination and then side by side, there'll be a Mad Hatters Tea Party affair with animals dressed in clothes talking on the telephone.

An Indian fortune teller told my fortune for free. He didn't like Charley at all apparently and said that the guy I was involved with at the moment was no good. I was highly amused. He gave me a small bead – a good luck charm.

I bought a little cassette player in Change Alley and six pirated tapes. Everyone who travelled overseas from Australia took advantage of the duty-free laws as back home the Australian government put "duty" – a large tax – on imports. Cameras, hi-fi systems, alcohol, tobacco… Singapore and Hong Kong were the major hubs of the duty-free perk. Pirated music was then, as now, illegal. Like a lot of things in South-East Asia, a blind eye was turned. Just a word to the shopkeeper and a minute later I was being shown boxes of copied tapes in a back room, a fraction of the high price back home. Pink Floyd, Bob Dylan, the Rolling Stones, Simon and Garfunkel, Neil Diamond, Cat Stevens… all the latest albums.

Soon *Dark Side of the Moon* joined joints and whisky as we whiled away the tropical nights.

*

Charley became my first boyfriend since parting with Ken three years before. They were polar opposites. I'd become so used to treading on eggshells around Ken it took a while to accept Charley's open friendliness. I was still trying to lose weight, and when Charley casually mentioned that he thought diets were ridiculous, my devotion was complete.

When I was 18 and still living at home, I started going out with Anton, a young Swiss guy who'd migrated to Australia alone in the mid-sixties. There was huge social pressure to settle down young back then, especially in Adelaide, which was like a large country town. Engaged at 18, married at 20, first baby by 22 was the norm. Anton was devoted, and planned our future together. However, after we'd been seeing each other for about a year, I started discovering lies he'd been telling me since day one.

Nothing drastic: he wasn't fleeing the law or any such thing. Just bullshit to big-note himself, lies about his life in Switzerland which couldn't be verified. The girlfriend who'd died in a car accident which precipitated his decision to come to Australia, the rock and roll band he'd played in – it turned out that I was his first-ever girlfriend, and he couldn't play a note. I was well impressed that he'd spent a day in trendy London as a stopover on the way to Australia, but his trip turned out to have been a direct flight from Geneva. On and on it went. I'd been brought up to be scrupulously honest – lying seemed to me beyond pointless, a sign of major insecurity.

He even tried to convince me his lying was justified – he'd been terribly lonely when he first arrived in Australia and the only way he could distract himself was to keep moving on. If he constantly lied to the new people he met, that meant he had to leave before being found out. If I couldn't understand and accept this, there was something wrong with *me*...

He told me he was part of a scam at his work as a motor mechanic. If a woman came in to have something simple done to her car like a service, he and the leading hand would tell her she needed a part replaced, charge her for the work which wasn't done, and pocket the money. Anton was delighted at this bottomless source of funds and he took it for granted that I would be too. I was disgusted.

Inevitably, we parted. My mother was devastated. I didn't tell her about Anton's darker side. She was desperate to marry me off. "You've wasted so much time," she lamented.

I was 20 years old.

First a compulsive liar, then a violent bully. Perhaps at last I had made a good choice in Charley.

Chapter 8

Malaysia was an emerging third-world country back in the seventies, suspicious of foreigners. We were given only a week on our entry stamps when we crossed the causeway from Singapore. We travelled by train north through green countryside for the whole afternoon before we got to our destination. Miles of rubber plantations reminded me of British colonial days. Little cups hung beneath incisions made in the bark of the rubber trees, collecting the latex as it slowly dripped in.

Malacca's Youth Hostel was right on the beach, surrounded by palm trees, but our laidback mood was short-lived. The previous month, the police had raided the place and turfed everyone out – charged with the dreadful crime of being a hippie. Charley's conservative short back and sides were growing on me fast... the following day we went to the immigration office to extend our visas and were given a lecture on how not to be a hippie. Perhaps the official wasn't impressed by my trendy new long pants, made from white cotton Malaysian flour bags.

Malacca was an intriguing mixture of architecture: Christchurch built by the Dutch in the 18th century, quaint Malay wooden houses up on stilts, and the Porta de Santiago which was part of the remains of a Portuguese fortress from 1511. The body of the Jesuit St Francis Xavier was once housed in Malacca in St Pauls, a Portuguese church now in ruins. Six months later, I was to see his relocated remains at St Francis's Exposition, which happens once every decade in Panjim in Goa in India, yet another former Portuguese colony. I was intrigued by the tiny body, surprisingly intact, clothed in richly embroidered robes. His right arm had been removed for display in Rome – obviously his most holy part as it had poured baptismal water on around 300,000 people across Asia.

In a few short days in Malacca I'd seen examples of three previous European colonial powers, all with their fingers in the pie of the Far East. Malay citizens of Chinese and Indian ancestry were evidence of Asian incursions. Perhaps the contemporary indigenous Malays had good reason to be less than welcoming towards foreigners.

We headed for Ipoh, a town on the west side of the Malaysian peninsula in the middle of limestone country. Getting from Malacca to Ipoh took a whole day: two buses, one taxi and we thumbed five lifts. Our reward at the New Princess Hotel was hot water, the first we'd had in all our accommodation since Darwin.

> Had a wash which was heaven, then went out for tea at some local open air restaurant complex. Had fried mee with egg, fruit curry, shellfish and peanut sauce, es buah, fresh fruit juice and coffee.
>
> We went out north of Ipoh to some limestone cliffs and saw some more cave-temples, one Chinese and two Indian. The Indian temples were very gaudy affairs, brightly painted with vivid statues, and pictures everywhere. One was a complete limestone cave with just the entrance built on. An Indian attendant put pink and white powder in the middle of our foreheads when we went inside. We had to go barefoot. We went clambering around a few caves which were generally very dirty with soot and rubbish and saw several small bats.

All the young Western women on the overland trail complained of being groped. As well as the predictable bottom-pinching in crowds, my experiences included being grabbed between the legs by a guy passing by in a park, and having my right breast squeezed by a hand out of a taxi window. Malaysia was no different.

Got a lift soon after in a truck. I sat in the cabin and Charley sat on the tray at the back, but the two Chinese were members of the Wandering Hands Society and I was getting really shat off and ended up belting both of them, much to their great amusement. They stopped to buy some durians and I climbed up with Charley.

Chapter 9

Charley's relaxed, easy-going nature belied his single-mindedness. He was heading for England, the land of his childhood, with $500 in his pocket, a modest amount even by frugal traveller standards.

"I need to get myself a perk," he said. And before too long he had one.

In Bangkok we were approached by a young Australian guy. "Do you want a student card?" he asked. International student cards were essential for cheap travel and all travellers, whether genuine students or not, got themselves this little money saver.

Charley laughed. "I'll take 50."

The following day Charley was set up. Blank student cards, glue, rubber stamps, ink-pad…his financial future secure for the moment. The prospective buyer would give Charley $5 US plus a photo, and the following day had their own officially stamped student card.

However, before long a cloud appeared on the horizon. The official providers of real student cards had complained to the authorities, and another young Australian guy also selling illegal cards ended up in a Bangkok prison. He'd been travelling at a similar pace to us and we'd met him every now and again. One of our group who visited him in prison told us horrific news – his Thai fellow-inmates were trying to inject him with heroin to get him addicted and have access to the money he'd need to support his habit. He was an innocent abroad, the same as the rest of us, lulled into a false sense that somehow being a Westerner in Asia made it ok to do things you'd never do at home.

I hoped the Australian Embassy could get him out, but never heard of his fate.

*

Bangkok had been a haven for US soldiers on Rest and Recreation leave at the height of the Vietnam War. In 1974, America's involvement in Vietnam was winding down and soldiers were no longer coming. The war had provided an income for thousands of bar girls but now only a handful still plied their trade along Patpong and Silom Roads. Bored go-go dancers at the Playboy strip club gyrated languidly to the music in front of a handful of patrons. They were slim, pretty and scantily clad. Every now and again, one would pop a white ping-pong ball out of her vagina over the edge of the stage, but even that failed to rev up the crowd.

The Malaysia Hotel in Bangkok was upmarket – modern with ensuite toilet and bathroom, air-conditioning, telephone and even a swimming pool. Once crammed with US soldiers, it now attracted overland travellers with its cheap rates and luxury. Charley and I moved in. The following day was Charley's birthday and I gave him a bottle of Mehkong whisky. Back in Australia, I'd been an occasional drinker, had only ever smoked a dozen cigarettes and had puffed on three or four joints of marijuana. Charley drank most evenings, smoked tobacco off and on, and indulged in dope whenever it was available.

"I'll have a consciousness-alterer every night if it's available," he laughed.

That day Charley sold five student cards. With money in his pocket, a joint in one hand and a glass of whisky in the other, he was having the perfect birthday.

*

I felt restless to keep moving and see what was around the next corner but Charley, disregarding his very limited funds, was cruising his way through Asia. He happily lazed for days in the same place, sometimes spending the whole day reading, music playing in the background. I put my own wishes aside and fell in with the pace of Charley's life. Perhaps it was my years of conditioning that girls must indulge the whims of males while ignoring their own. Or perhaps I sensed that Charley was doing his own thing; if I'd said I wanted to travel faster, he wouldn't have come with me. Was I just along for the ride?

One of the things which had attracted me to Charley in the first place was his independence – after the stifling insecurity of my two former boyfriends Charley's confidence was a breath of fresh air. But sometimes I felt that the pendulum had swung too much in the opposite direction.

I made slight concessions if I didn't feel like hanging around and took myself off sightseeing while Charley read.

*

Buddha sticks of marijuana were on offer in Thailand, a stronger version of that available thus far. I didn't like the stronger grass. Instead of feeling happy and carefree, I'd sometimes find myself feeling anxious.

Despite this, I still kept Charley company whenever he indulged in this particular "consciousness-alterer", but just had one or two puffs.

The first day we arrived in Bangkok, we did what all travellers did and went to the Poste Restante section of the main post office where we both had five letters waiting for us. Writing and receiving letters was a big part of travelling. Phone calls were prohibitively expensive, and even though letters both to and from home often went astray, it was the only way to find out what was happening. Charley and I had both had money forwarded by our families and spent several hours retrieving our funds from the bank. This glacial pace of Asian banks was soon accepted as the norm, and having money sent every couple of months was unavoidable as carrying big amounts of cash was too risky. The travellers' cheques and cash I'd brought from Australia were just about gone.

One of Charley's letters contained a cheque from the older American woman who had spilled her stuff into the mud in Timor. Earlier on she'd been called back to Darwin unexpectedly by her business partner and didn't have enough cash on her for the fare. Having money sent from Australia would have taken forever. Charley had been travelling with her through Timor and readily offered to lend her the money. I thought this was very good of him, considering his parlous financial state, and the fact they'd only recently met. He must have been a good judge of character – not only did she repay the original loan, she regularly sent him modest cheques which turned up along the Hippie Trail. I was to see many such examples of Charley's seemingly innate talent to attract good fortune. He told me one of his friends back in Hobart used to say to him, "Bend over Charley and let the sun shine out."

Bangkok was an endless source of fascination. We wandered through Buddhist temples covered with brilliant porcelain tiles resembling fish scales, amongst hordes of golden buddhas with the occasional black one for good measure and ended up at the Wat Pho where the Reclining Buddha has his abode. Describing him as a "beached whale" is very close.

All this beauty amongst hideous noise and air pollution with kamikaze drivers who only survived because the traffic was generally at a stand-still...

Went to the Snake Farm to see venom being extracted. There were banded kraits and king cobras which were being force fed, and ordinary cobras which were being "milked" by allowing them to bite a glass dish. The attendants were very game and handled the snakes very casually. The cobras put up their hood when annoyed and look very impressive with their heart shaped pattern on the back of their head.

One snake had swallowed two thirds of another and they just pulled it out and it slithered off wet but otherwise fine. They produce the anti-venene by injecting increasing amounts of venom into horses over a period of several months.

Our doses of culture were tempered by eating our way around open air markets. I raised the tone of my increasingly tatty wardrobe with an Indian cheesecloth dress, the height of hippie fashion.

Not all Westerners were having such a good time – we met a fresh-faced young English guy who'd been befriended by a teenage local who was showing him round and sharing his room. When he told his young guide he was leaving the following day, the boy asked him several times, "You go tomorrow?" The next morning, the English guy awoke to find his new "friend" gone, along with his watch, travellers' cheques and cash. He didn't seem too concerned. There hadn't been much cash so in reality he'd only lost his watch and the time taken to replace his cheques. It was hard to be judgemental given the gulf between the lifestyles of South East Asia and the west.

Civil unrest eventually drove us out of our comfort zone. Six civilians were killed in riots by police one night, and ten more the next. It was time to go.

Chapter 10

We crossed the Mekong River and ended up in Vientiane, the capital of Laos. Even though the Vietnam War had spilled over into Laos, a ceasefire was in place around Vientiane. Soldiers in different uniforms wandered the streets amicably. Apparently three months earlier the two military factions, one the neutralist-rightists from the Mekong River valley surrounding Vientiane and the other the pro-Communist Pathet Lao from the north, had come to some peaceful agreement and formed a coalition government. Prior to this, a visa to Laos was impossible to get.

Vientiane was unbelievably hot and humid. Our room at the Saylom Villa didn't have a fan and we soon moved into a mixed dormitory which had one. Although the French were long gone, their influence lingered and we bought French bread, tomatoes, cucumber, pineapple, bananas and spring onions at the markets – the first decent bread we'd had since Darwin four months earlier.

Before long, Charley had sniffed out the local opium den behind our villa, officially illegal but ignored. We were shown through a wooden door by a tiny wizened old Lao guy straight out of the movies. He beckoned us to come in quickly and shut the door behind us. We entered a sparsely furnished darkened room.

> You lie on a wooden "bed" with your head on a wooden pallet and inhale until your lungs are filled then exhale straight away. A small lump of opium resin is heated over a lamp flame then stuck to the bowl of the pipe (on the outside). Small pieces are taken off with a skewer and put into the bowl through a small hole in the top. The bowl plus opium is heated over the flame and the smoke inhaled at the same time.

The languid dreamy effect of the opiate was somewhat tempered by nausea, common with novice smokers, apparently... Back in our dormitory a Western guy with thick shaggy black hair and beard lay on his bed in an opium haze, continually scratching himself, another side-effect of opium.

Heard some horrifying news tonight. A bus from Luang Prabang was ambushed by Meo tribesmen, formerly trained by the US CIA, and two Westerners and two Lao were killed, including the driver. An Australian girl was wounded. The two Westerners killed in the ambush were the brother and sister-in-law of the Australian Ambassador to Laos.

The Ambassador had encouraged his brother and his wife to sit up front to get the best views of the jungle. A French girl in the dormitory read the details out loud from the newspaper. She was in an agitated state. She had bought a ticket for that bus but had overslept. We were all uneasy – travelling was supposed to be fun. No-one expected armed tribesmen to leap out of the jungle and spray a local bus with bullets from US-supplied weapons.

Charley and I planned to travel north to Luang Prabang. We figured the assailants would be long gone and a few days later headed for the bus station at six am. However, the bus didn't turn up and even though I was nervous of flying, I was so relieved to catch the little Royal Air Lao Electra – although economy was full and we had to go first class, another first for both of us. It only took half an hour and we flew north into the little town right up in the green cloud-covered mountains.

Went for a walk along the Mekong, past the Royal Palace and a couple of wats. I'm very impressed with the town, especially as it was nice and cool until about 10 am. Climbed Phousi in the late afternoon. It's a frangipani-covered hill in the centre of town, with dozens of very steep steps leading to the temple on top.

There's a beautiful view from the top – the two rivers, surrounding mountains, the town in the river valley – and everything is so green.

Drove 35 kilometres or so to see the waterfalls at Kuang Si. Went with three other Australians and two French. Very pretty countryside on the way. The waterfalls are beautiful – very high with lots of streams running into deep pools at their base. We climbed about half-way up and got soaked looking round some caves behind the falls. Just like the movies. The rock formations of the falls are very unusual – structures looking like inverted bowls jut out from the side of the cliff and the water cascades over them. It started raining and finished off the job that the spray started. We climbed across the face of the waterfall and eventually got right to the top.

We could see a shelter in the rice paddies on the other side of the stream above the falls, and headed across to get out of the rain. Halfway over, I slipped on the slimy rocks beneath the water. The stream, though shallow, flowed quickly and carried me over the slippery rocks towards the drop. I stopped a couple of metres from the edge. My angel was still on duty. On the way back we were walking along a path when we heard what sounded like a gun-shot, and the grass 20 metres on whistled and parted. We all looked at each other. "Was that a shot?" We carried on through the dense vegetation, not particularly concerned. The whole scene had an air of unreality, possibly helped by the several joints shared during the afternoon.

> Two days later we visited a couple of villages: Saw a big pile of bomb shells, broken guns etc in one village. Both had palm trees minus tops – reminder of the war. Apparently they were evacuated to Luang Prabang before the bombing and a lot of huts were destroyed.

The war in Laos was referred to as the "secret war" as the US and North Vietnamese governments had signed agreements which specified the neutrality of Laos. From the destruction we had seen, it was apparently one of the world's worst kept secrets. The following year, 1975, the Pathet Lao and North Vietnamese gained control of Laos, eliminating the monarchy. The country is now described as a single-party socialist republic.

Surviving the Seventies

*

After three weeks in Laos, we were back in northern Thailand in Chiang Mai. A local eating place, Pats, was the place to be and the outdoor tables lit by lanterns were always crammed with travellers. I started with a huge bowl of soup, then had noodles piled with the usual stir-fried fresh vegetables and cashews, and finished off with fruit salad. I felt guilty when Charley commented on my huge appetite that evening.

I posted a little blue cotton shirt with elephants on it in a brown-paper parcel back home to Danny in Adelaide. You weren't supposed to include letters in parcels – they were to be sent by the dearer letter rate. I wrote a little note and slipped it into the pocket of the shirt. Charley encouraged me to send presents home. His father had been away a lot in the navy when he was a kid living in England. "We used to love getting the parcels my father sent back home to us. They were always full of amazing stuff from exotic places in the Far East."

We headed south back to Bangkok and went to see Thai boxing.

The boxers go through a fascinating ritual at the beginning of each match, religious by all appearances. They kneel and bow with their heads to the floor – really psyching themselves up. They go through very controlled, graceful movements – rather like ballet dancers, as part of their ritual. Each boxer has his own personal performance. They box in time to music produced by a tambourine I think. The first round is slow, then quickens towards the end. Their movements are very graceful – they look more like dancers than boxers in their initial round. We saw five matches, each of five four-minute rounds. It wasn't nearly as brutal as I'd imagined even though they use feet, knees and fists. The place was packed – lord knows how the locals can afford the seats which range from 45–150 baht.

We'd been away from Bangkok so long that Charley had ten letters from home waiting for him in poste restante, and I had nine. We sat in a café reading the interesting bits out to each other. My mother doted on Danny and her letters were always full of grandmotherly news.

Halfway through her latest letter I looked up at Charley. "I've got to go home."

I'd been aware for some time that my youngest brother was causing Mum some worry. He was 13 years old and always seemed to be in trouble. After years of poor health, my father had died the previous year leaving mum with my youngest brother and my sister who was now 17. My two brothers closer to me in age no longer lived at home. Mum had been called to the local school to sort out yet another escapade and was at the end of her tether. She felt caring for Danny was getting too much for her and asked if I could come back earlier than the six months we'd originally planned.

I rang home reverse charges that evening. Mum wasn't well. She suffered from a hiatus hernia which made her feel nausea on occasion and was feeling particularly ill when I spoke to her. I said I'd be back as soon as the money for my fare turned up.

I felt ok about going home. My original plan had been to travel for six months, return to Adelaide from wherever I happened to be, then fly with Danny to London which had always been my real destination. Initially I'd been against taking children to Asia, concerned about all the terrible exotic diseases but I'd been surprised at the number of Western kids on the Hippie Trail – apart from the gastric problems we all had from time to time, they were fine.

Even though we'd always known we'd be parting somewhere along the trail, Charley and I got a shock when we realised I'd be going a month sooner than expected. We revised our plans. After spending some time with my family and catching up with friends, I would fly back to Asia rather than London. Charley planned to do the long Everest Base Camp trek in Nepal in October when the monsoon was over, and I would meet him there in Kathmandu.

Advertisements cluttered the notice board at the Malaysia Hotel, pushing everything the promoters hoped would appeal to travellers on the cheap. *Siam Travel News*, run by a young Australian guy, offered Thai International tickets to Sydney for two-thirds of the regular price. Airline prices were generally fixed worldwide in the seventies and bargains were rare.

Our farewell dinner was at The Pub, so-named to attract the travelling fraternity. Charley shouted me out, which was very good of him considering his precarious finances. We talked a lot and enjoyed ourselves – it didn't seem sad like a proper goodbye. After all, we'd be back together in a month or so.

*

The following evening, I was in the air heading south back to Australia. Thai International was, then as now, an upmarket airline.

> I was definitely the scrappiest in the lounge – everyone else was in their six inch heels and carrying their Samsonite luggage. Had a lovely meal of orange juice, filet mignon steak with cheese sauce and stuffed capsicum and side

salad, hot roll with butter, fruit custard in pastry for dessert, then cheese and biscuits and tea. What a spread!

Some things have been sacrificed in the current airline price wars...
　I landed in Sydney just as dawn was breaking.

Chapter 11

Danny and I stood on a crowded wooden balcony in Kathmandu and watched the celebration of the Living Goddess pass by. Ordinarily I would have been transfixed by this procession from an ancient world, but I couldn't lift my flat feelings. I'd been in the city for a day. Charley wasn't at the Ganga Lodge where we'd arranged to meet, and there was no letter at the post office. He may not have received my letters with our new travel details, the postal system in Asia being so bad. Had he left for India, the next country on our planned route? After six weeks apart, I'd been so looking forward to meeting up again and picking up where we'd left off.

> It's taken the edge off the pleasure I otherwise would have got from Kathmandu, with its

quaint windy streets and higgledy piggledy houses all crammed together. Goats and cows wander at random through the streets which are filled with people and dozens of children. Danny has made a friend here at the Lodge and we went with her and her mother tonight to see a procession of the Goddess, Kumari Devi, a young girl who is replaced at the first signs of puberty. The occasional dragon and monster and band made it interesting for the kids. The people whose balcony we watched from were very kind and friendly. Their house is funny – narrow little low doorways and cramped little staircases. Most houses here seem to be two or three storeys high.

The little girl, about ten years old, all dressed up in finery, sat solemnly in a massive wooden cart as it was dragged through the narrow streets. It must have been incomprehensible to her – one day she was an ordinary Nepalese girl, the next worshipped as a goddess.

A *kumari* is a young unmarried girl, *devi* is divine female energy, and she is revered as the reincarnation of the Hindu goddess *Durga*. She is chosen from the caste of silver and goldsmiths in a procedure rivalling the selection of the Dalai Lama in Tibet. This state of elevation remains only until she begins menstruating, whereupon she finds herself back in her previous life. This however is no reprieve. Apparently no-one is too keen to marry a former goddess as legend has it her husband will die soon after. In a society where marriage back in the 1970s was the only pathway for girls, her future appeared bleak. In reality, most former goddesses do marry, though later than usual for Nepalese girls. When this elevated position becomes vacant, another pre-pubescent girl is chosen to take her place.

Charley and I had originally planned to meet up in the middle of October when he returned from his trek to the Everest Base Camp. This was now two weeks away. Back in Adelaide I'd got a letter saying he'd decided to go on a shorter trek and would be in Kathmandu sooner. Consequently I changed my plans and wrote telling him of my earlier arrival date. I could only assume he hadn't got this letter and was expecting me mid-month, and had gone elsewhere in the meantime. I left letters at the post office and the desk of the guest house; it was all I could do.

Kathmandu was an easy place to forget one's troubles. It was like a medieval city. Other Asian cities had been transformed by the worst of the west – massive freeways, traffic-jammed vehicles, constant pollution, shoddy buildings. You had to search for the old way of life in the back streets and alleyways. Here it was in your face. Ancient buildings predominated, with tiny doorways where you had to stoop to pass through.

The appeal of the place has been enough to raise my spirits out of sight. This morning we got up early and cycled into town looking at the temples round Durbar Square. We saw the residence of the Goddess with its unusual balcony where she appears from time to time. Also the Hanuman Dhoka with the monkey god cloaked in red, the Taleju Temple with its four stupas, the Kal Bhairbab with the image of the goddess of terror, Kali, where animal sacrifices are made, and the Akash Bhairab with a huge image of a face of sorts. Some of the most interesting temples we've seen so far on the trip. They're very old and built of dark bricks and wood generally, and in pagoda style. The square is used as a market place and is teeming with vendors early in the morning.

Even though there are lots of westerners in Kathmandu, it's surprisingly un-touristy. There are none of the usual dozen signs directing you to the places of interest – in fact it's quite the opposite and even with a map you're not quite sure you're in the right place. The weather's been glorious – lovely sunny days and no humidity. The nights even tend to be a bit on the cold side.

Occasionally you can even get a glimpse of the snow-covered Himalayas to the north when the clouds lift over the range surrounding the valley.

The first time I saw human faeces on the side of the road, I thought it was dog poo. It didn't take long to realise that it wasn't, and that it was everywhere. It hadn't occurred to me that perhaps most people were too poor to have an inside toilet. Backyard dunnies didn't seem to exist, and I saw no public toilets. I later learned that Hindus consider having eating and toilet arrangements under the same roof unclean. One had to take care given the hippie fashion of long pants with trailing cuffs, and wrap-around skirts dragging through the dirt.

One English girl was tottering along on platform clogs, the height of fashion back home but quite a feat here given the unevenness of the roads.

I laughed. "Why on earth are you wearing those here?"

"It keeps me above the shit," she replied, poker-faced.

Kathmandu was like a permanent fun-park for kids. I hired a bicycle every day and Danny sat on the back as I pedalled the pot-holed streets, dodging goats and chickens. We visited the zoo with its predictably small cages for very big animals – yaks, deer, Himalayan bears and tigers.

Went out to the Swayambhu Monkey Temple. What a fascinating place! Monkeys literally everywhere, rolling down the hand-rails of the stairs, swinging through the trees, climbing all over the temple buildings and statues. One tried to grab my bag and I had visions of all my papers being scattered through the tree-tops. Danny was very good and walked up and down the huge staircase and all around the temple. It's right on top of a hill and gives a wonderful view of the valley and nearby mountains with their steppe-farming.

Our guesthouse was in the same building as a school and Danny played with the kids every afternoon. They were fascinated by his little shoulder bag filled with plastic toy animals and in no time half its contents had disappeared into the throng. Danny didn't seem to mind, and I was happy the local kids now had at least one toy.

There was a pile of bricks near the wall next to the guesthouse. After school the local kids played on the bricks and sat on top of the wall, which was taller than me. I told Danny to be careful but he slipped off the top and landed in the mud on the other side. From the indentation in the ground and the mud on his head, it was pretty obvious where he'd landed. I spent an anxious afternoon imaging how the Kathmandu hospital would handle a brain haemorrhage, but he was no worse for wear. On another occasion, I was taking a photo of him perched on the back of the bike when it toppled over, depositing him on the footpath. I was out of practice at being a parent.

Freak Street was the local travellers' haunt, crammed with food shops selling a mixture of Asian and western food at ridiculously low prices. The locals were quick to adapt to Western tastes, and dope smokers with the munchies were abundantly catered for. Marijuana was everywhere. Kathmandu was the hippie Mecca, the in-place on the overland trail. Psychedelically dressed, long-haired... some stayed for months in a permanently stoned haze.

One meal, "Joe's Special", stands out. *What a spread! Potato, rice, noodles, vegetables galore plus eggs and meat*, I wrote in my journal.

Much to my delight, I now weighed 10 stone 3 pounds, a whole 11 pounds lighter than when I'd left Adelaide the first time. This didn't seem likely to last.

*

Assuming Charley wasn't expecting me till mid-October I took Danny by bus to Pokhara, 200 kilometres to the west, on a huge lake surrounded by

Himalayan peaks. We got a typical basic little room at the Hotel Snow Land, close by the lake and safer for Danny away from the traffic.

> He's outside with a bunch of Nepalese kids at the moment, throwing rocks and sticks at a passing herd of cows and buffaloes. I should stop him, but all the local kids do it, so it's a bit hard to explain. The animals seem fairly unconcerned, as it's the local way of herding them.

Nepal was a never-ending source of playmates, and western kids were immediately accepted. The language barrier didn't exist. I doubt whether contraception was available in Nepal in the 1970s, and from the obvious poverty I assumed the infant mortality rate would be high. Before we left Australia, we'd been immunised against smallpox, cholera and typhoid, and Danny had a TB injection. I had gamma globulin injections against hepatitis A in Kathmandu. I took malaria tablets and Danny had his medication in a sweet syrup. All this was on top of the tetanus, polio, diphtheria and whooping cough inoculations which were standard for Australian children. There were basic clinics in Nepal, but I doubted the government would supply free immunisation, and the locals could never have paid. This was classic Darwinian survival of the fittest.

Children were also expected to work from a young age – herding animals, fetching water, looking after younger siblings, weeding, planting and harvesting in the fields. I never saw an overweight Nepalese kid. They'd walk up precipitous slopes carrying huge cans of water, without batting an eyelid.

Danny caught some gastric illness while we were in Pokhara. He had a temperature one night, followed by diarrhoea for four days before I finally gave him Lomotil medication. The standard practice was to let nature take its course to allow your body to build up resistance, but I figured it was now time to give nature a helping hand.

When he was on the mend I hired a local wooden canoe and meandered all over the place trying to get the hang of Nepalese paddling techniques before eventually getting out to the island in the middle of the lake. The water was clean and deep and shark-free, perfect for swimming though rather fresh from the melting snow.

Back in Kathmandu, we went straight to the post office and found a letter from Charley. An immense weight fell from my shoulders. It turned out we'd actually been in Pokhara at the same time for two days. We hopped straight into a rickshaw and got pedalled to the G.C. Lodge. I hauled my pack up the several flights of stairs to Charley's room which was on the top floor. I knocked while trying to catch my breath.

Charley was his usual laidback self. "It's about time," he said as he opened the door, the familiar grin lighting up his face.

I'd been a bit worried about whether Charley and Danny would get along. Charley was the eldest of three kids and had migrated from Britain to Australia with his family in his teens. He wasn't used to small children. I needn't have been concerned. Charley always made time to play with Danny, reading to him whenever a book was poked under his nose and he even taught him the alphabet and numbers. They drifted into a close, easy-going relationship.

The biggest obstacle with Danny was that he didn't like walking. He had plenty of energy, running around with the Nepalese kids all day, but when it came to walking to a café or bus station, he suddenly demanded to be carried. At three, most Nepalese kids were carrying a younger sibling on one hip. We compromised. Sometimes we made him walk and put up with the whingeing, at other times we carted him along. He was no light weight, pretty solid and big for his age. I should have thought of this in terms of a work-out, but the current obsession with exercise didn't exist in my world back in the seventies.

Chapter 12

Hippie buses plied their trade between Nepal and Europe, driving passengers in both directions. From Nepal, they headed south to India, then west through Pakistan, Afghanistan, Iran and Turkey into Greece. Real travellers looked down their noses at this up-market comfort. The only way was to do it hard, on local buses, trains and boats.

However after so many months on the road, we decided we could bend the rules a little and boarded *The Rocket*, bound for Delhi, for $22 US. It was an old English passenger bus and had been travelling this route for 13 months, which may have had some bearing on what followed over the next five days. We left Kathmandu four hours late, broke a side rear-vision mirror side-swiping something, then the windscreen shattered on a toll-gate boom which was lowered as we drove through. Charley, Danny and I were sitting right behind the driver who drove with a bandana around his face like a bandit. In no time my hair was like straw. Roads in Nepal cling to the mountainsides with vertical drops inches from your wheels. One develops a certain fatalistic attitude.

We passed through Lumbini, Buddha's birthplace, but he wasn't smiling on us as the exhaust manifold fell off. We boiled the billy over a campfire by the side of the road and drank tea for several hours while it was repaired. No sooner had we got to the next town than an electric fire broke out and now the bus had to be push-started.

> Got ourselves through the yards of red tape both sides of the border. Our first sight in India was about 50 vultures tearing a dead dog to pieces. Not a very good first impression! The Indian countryside is very flat and dry hereabouts and not very impressive after the scenery of Nepal. No sign of poverty so far – the people are very numerous and all appear healthy. Danny's been incredibly good, playing quietly with his toys or looking at his books. No trouble at all. I haven't even had to entertain him much. Stopped outside Faizabad for the night and slept on the bus again.

There were countless mosquitoes around and poor Danny got eaten alive. They don't seem to bother him though and don't itch.

Continued on through very bad traffic conditions – everyone seems to drive or wander down the middle of the road, and there are cows every few yards. It's a real concentration effort to drive among it all. John the driver did a very good job and didn't run anyone over which was amazing. I've been very impressed with what I've seen so far – no shit on the streets. Stopped at a Tourist Bungalow in Lucknow for the night and slept in a dormitory. Seems a nice enough town with a lot of buildings which look like mosques.

Actually made it to Delhi by driving a couple of hours in the dark with and without lights. However they held out till we arrived for which everyone was very grateful. A very pleasant trip which is surprising considering all the problems we experienced. The seats were very comfortable with plenty of leg room and the three beds at the back were handy for putting Danny to sleep.

Took ourselves to a guest house called Mrs Dunkeleys which was beyond belief. I still haven't recovered. Had to ascend several flights of very dark stairs into a very smelly lounge room which was due to a combination of half a dozen dogs lying around the place and the countless mattresses along the side of the hall. We were warned about the rats which was rather disconcerting. The room we were shown was a hovel with a dirty floor, collapsing beds and filthy holey mattresses. I've never seen such a dump. However at that hour of the night we had no choice. I saw about six rats while lying down with Danny and scared them off by hitting the floor. Charley and I repaired our shattered nerves by taking half a mandrax each and smoking hash while sitting on the front doorstep.

Charley went out early next morning to find alternative accommodation, in a very bad mood as the rats had eaten two holes in his beloved leather shoulder bag. We escaped from Mrs Dunkeleys to the Crown Hotel, locally known as the Shooting Gallery for reasons soon apparent.

> It's a very interesting part of the city here in Old Delhi. We're in the market area and there are dozens of fruit and vegetable sellers all over the place and countless little shops and stalls, and the usual number of cows wandering the streets.

Pamela Irving

Had a very frustrating morning. Went to the Old Delhi station to get our tickets to Agra and Bombay only to find the student concession office was at the New Delhi station. Tracked over there to find the concession office closed until Saturday as this a public holiday. Smoked some hash in the taxi en route to the hotel and got caught in the most unbelievable traffic jam consisting mostly of cows, carts and people. I got the most claustrophobic feeling among the sea of faces and felt that all of India was about to descend upon us.

We'd hardly got back to our room when a bearded Western face with straggly hair stuck his head through the broken upper panel of our door.

"Morphiiine?" he enquired in an accent unmistakably French, dragging out the last syllable.

Charley, ever the dabbler, was soon bargaining across our rickety table. The French guy shook some white powder onto a sheet of paper. Charley agreed to buy half, whereupon the dealer produced a razor blade and divided the little pile. He pushed one part towards Charley.

"Are they both the same?" Charley asked. To our untrained eyes, the pile closest to the dealer was obviously the larger of the two.

"Yes, yes, the same," he quickly replied.

"In that case, I'll have the other one," countered Charley.

This led to a re-combining and re-division of the morphine.

Was this a glimpse of the lengths addicts went to in order to support their habit?

The dreamy, relaxed feeling was similar to the effect we'd had from the opium we'd tried in Laos.

*

It's a holiday period at present and we saw a ceremony one evening in which three giant effigies of Rama were burnt amid countless fireworks. Last night we saw a procession of sorts from our hotel – elephants and all, but didn't find out the purpose behind it.

After dragging his heels through South East Asia, Charley was now in a mood to move much more quickly. His enthusiasm for travelling overland all the way to Europe was waning, and he was inclined to blame me for this change of heart. Hanging around in Nepal waiting for me to return had frustrated him and he now felt like making up for lost time. Perhaps he wasn't aware of the frustration I'd felt previously, always moving at his glacial pace.

"Hey, steady on." I spread my arms in indignation. "You told me you were going to the Everest Base Camp and you'd be away for six weeks, then you changed your mind and ended up only trekking for ten days." I felt my voice rising. "*Then* you went off to Pokhara and didn't leave me a letter in Kathmandu, even though you *knew* I'd be there soon. Even the letter you sent me to Adelaide didn't have any dates in it, so I had no idea when you'd be back in Kathmandu. When I arrived I thought you were off somewhere else in Nepal."

There was nothing underhand in Charley's vagueness, just typical male lack of attention to detail, but my feelings that I didn't figure strongly in Charley's decision making were strengthened. But perhaps we were both ready for a change. It was now November, and we'd left Australia in March. A lot of months of experiencing both the highs and lows of travel on the cheap.

*

Seeing the Taj Mahal ghostly in the light of the full moon was the best way to rekindle the flame. It's still the most amazing building I've seen. Moghul Emperor Shah Jehan built it as a mausoleum for his wife Mumtaz Mahal, who died in childbirth while delivering their 14th baby. To someone who'd only had one child, going through labour 14 times was beyond reality. I felt Mumtaz deserved every speck of the pale glossy marble.

Legend has it that Shah Jehan intended to build a black marble version of the Taj for himself on the opposite side of the river, connecting the two by a bridge. True or not, it couldn't have come to pass as he spent his final eight years in the Agra Fort, imprisoned by his third son, Aurangzeb. I've always felt a vague sense of disappointment over this.

> Agra itself is a very much more interesting town than I'd anticipated. It's a real zoo here with buffaloes, cows, camels, donkeys, horses, goats, pigs etc etc wandering all over the place. Danny's most impressed as zoos are about his favourite place. They pile the animals with incredible loads here. I wonder their backs don't break. There are lots of very cheap marble goods – from jewellery boxes to chessboards. We resisted temptation and just looked. We can see the Taj from our hotel floor, or part of it should I say.

Our plans were to travel to Bombay, then catch the ferry south to Goa, the former Portuguese enclave, and current hippie paradise. Charley was going to stay a month then return to Bombay and fly to

London. His finances were getting very low. Danny and I were going to stay on in Goa for another month to avoid the worst of the British winter and then join Charley in London. We almost didn't get to first base as we literally couldn't get on the train in Delhi. We were caught in a fighting throng which is the only way the Indians were assured of a seat. Dozens of people with dozens of packages shoving as if possessed. I can still picture a skinny little middle-aged Indian man all dressed in white being shoved through a carriage window by his family who'd come to see him off. We can't say we weren't warned.

All the travellers heading towards Australia took great delight in describing Indian train trips. Charley was ready to head for the airport and fly straight to London.

Our plans just about came unstuck again while on the train, travelling through Rajasthan at night towards Bombay.

> A group of police descended upon us looking for drugs which was most disconcerting as Charley had grass, hash and morphine in his red wash bag in the top of his pack. They really meant business and gave Charley a fairly thorough body search before starting on my shoulder bag. Fortunately they spilled most of my jewellery so I made a fuss and in all the

confusion was able to remove Charley's bag from the top of the pack which they'd just opened, and drop it on the floor. Somehow I got it under the seat which was difficult as the space was occupied by half a dozen trunks. I was sure I'd be noticed but our luck held out. I nearly died a thousand deaths when they came into the carriage. I'd worked so hard getting us to Goa and it all passed before my eyes that we were never going to get there. Charley languishing in some hole of an Indian jail for months and me outside kicking myself for being so stupid and careless.

In the cold light of day, in reality all the police were after was a bribe. We were later told that when the Bombay train stopped for a break in that particular town in Rajasthan, the police often searched westerners who they knew were on their way to Goa. A few discreetly offered rupees later, the journey would be resumed as if nothing had happened.

*

We hung over the rails and watched Bombay disappear behind us as we embarked on the 600 kilometre voyage south to Goa. After the chaos of Indian trains, it was great to be back at sea away from the throngs and the heat. The ship was even reasonably neat and new, in contrast to the rust-buckets we'd been on in Indonesia.

Like Kathmandu, Goa was the place to be on the overland trail. Formerly a Portuguese enclave, it was now a state of the Republic of India. Palm trees fringed the sandy beaches, the sea was calm, brightly painted sailing boats lay beached on the shore. Little fishing villages supplemented their meagre income by renting out whole houses for around $1 US a night, taking advantage of the hippie hordes which by now had been descending upon them for several years.

Reminders of the Portuguese history were everywhere. Goa was a little sea of Catholics in a huge ocean of Hindus. Our landlord was a young guy who looked Indian but was called Antonio Fernandez. He slept in a room at the back of the house while his mother and sister slept in another small building in the back yard. Chickens pecked around our feet. One afternoon we came back from the beach to find one of the chickens with its head caught beneath the door of the family kitchen. It was in a very awkward position as the rest of its body was upright. No doubt it had been trying to peck food scraps off the floor. We gently eased its head free, and it wobbled off no worse for wear.

It felt weird to have a place of my own again. I'd left my previous rented home nearly 12 months earlier. What a contrast to the semi-detached in Mosman. White-washed walls, a big front verandah, two bedrooms, a living room and kitchen, surrounded by sand and palm trees. The toilet was way down the backyard, just a couple of stones for your feet and a sloping base, made private with lattice walls of woven palm fronds. I hadn't expected a flushing system, but there was no can or long-drop like Australian backyard dunnies. What happened to it all?

We soon found out. Whenever one visited the loo, a couple of very large grey pot-bellied pigs turned up a few seconds later and started fighting their way in. A couple of strategically placed whacking sticks were used to keep them at bay. These were Goa's garbage disposal units, and very enthusiastic they were too. We were warned not to eat pork because of a parasite it contained. This warning was entirely superfluous.

Water was drawn from a well which was shared by the locals who all had a brass pot which was tied to a rope and lowered down. We didn't want to spend money on one of these very expensive items, so made do with a pottery one which had to be treated with care. One western guy didn't tie his brass pot securely to the rope and lost it in the depths. A villager descended into the well like a spider, hands and feet on the walls, and retrieved the pot. The owner didn't pay him the agreed sum, which unfortunately was not atypical of the attitude of some of the travellers on the cheap. Watching every cent became second-nature when limited funds had to last a year or more, but some took it to extremes and bragged about how little they could live on.

The locals were very blasé about the wells. The one we used had a typical wall around it, about waist height. However, when they were no longer used for whatever reason, the wall wasn't maintained. We were walking to the beach with our European neighbours and their little girl Carlie when we turned to see the kids who'd been trailing along behind standing on the edge of a nearby empty well peering down into the depths, the wall once around it long gone. Perhaps the local kids just grew up knowing the dangers.

Our little village, Calangute, was perfect. A short walk in one direction through low sand dunes and palms took us to the beach, in the other direction lay the road to the centre of the village where the open-air market supplied us with fresh fruit, vegetables, meat and fish. A huge pile of prawns cost two rupees, a pittance. We bought a few cooking pots, plates and cutlery and cooked over an open fire on the kitchen floor. When the fire was a bit too hot, you merely raised the rope tied to the handle of the cooking pot to reduce the heat to a simmer. I found this novelty all good fun. It was months since I'd cooked anything. We also got ourselves a kerosene lamp, the electricity supply being very erratic.

For kindling, we collected bits of palm fronds which fell to the ground below each tree. One day I'd just returned with a handful when Anthony knocked on the back door.

"Please don't take the leaves from under the trees," he said. "All the trees belong to different families and no-one else can take anything from them."

Even though dozens of coconut palms were scattered throughout and around the village, an ancient system of ownership applied which was respected without question.

No doubt we ignoramuses broke lots of local rules. We decided washing our hair at home required too much hauling of water, and headed for the well with our clay pot and shampoo. Charley poured water over my head, I lathered up, he poured more water and I rinsed off over the nearby grass. Later Anthony asked us to be careful not to pollute the well with shampoo. Perhaps the water table was close to the surface, or perhaps hair-washing was something one did behind closed doors.

One day we came back to find our verandah swept clean of all the dust and leaves which had been accumulating. I must have been lowering the tone of the neighbourhood. I'd made a half-hearted effort – the little bundle of twigs tied together which passed for a broom soon wore me out. I'd seen the local women wielding the brooms with great gusto. Perhaps that's what I lacked. Charley of course wouldn't have been expected to do any housework.

I wondered on occasion what they thought of us taking Danny covered in dirt from playing all day to the beach for a swim-cum-wash. The Indian kids were all neat and clean once out in public. A lot of westerners sunbathed naked on the sand which wasn't a local custom but it was tolerated. Sari-clad Indian holiday makers walked past on the beach, but appeared to ignore the bare white bodies. India was such a mixture of religions and customs, perhaps tolerance was ingrained.

In a strange coincidence, many years later when I was back in Adelaide working for a big private pathology company, we got a new employee in the laboratory – a young Indian guy from our village in Goa, Calangute.

*

Goa even supplied us with a playgroup for Danny. A Dutch woman, Mary, opened up her large house to all the hippie kids. Here Danny played with Lotus, Dolma, Kun-sang, Sai-wan, Ananda, Uriel, Elthira, Tiana, Hopi, Carlie, Rufus and Rainbow, all long-haired, scantily clad, adorned with coloured beads. In no time, Danny had various charms around his neck. He, Tommy and Jerome were the only kids with straight names. Here I had my first taste of home-made peanut butter, laboriously made with local peanuts, using a mortar and pestle. Back to basics was part of the appeal.

I'm turning into a first-class slob living in this idyllic place. If I have a swim most days I figure that's enough washing, and my hair is like straw. Food is easily prepared as we've got a Primus now and there's very little housework - getting water from the well is the hardest thing I do each day. We've fallen into a routine of sorts. Monday to Wednesday, Danny goes to Play School from 10 am to 12.30 so I get a peaceful morning. I'm meant to help out one morning per week which is fine by me. Thursday the school goes to Anjuna Beach in Mary's van, and Friday to Sunday we're on our own. We've been going to the beach late each afternoon and staying till the sun goes down. The sea is to the west here and we've seen some lovely sunsets. We've also been following the phases of the moon – the only constructive thing we've done in months. The new moon rises early and the waning moon late. Fancy not knowing that, or that the moon wanes after it is full.

Saw an interesting sight three nights ago, the night of the full moon. We came outside after earlier watching it rise from the beach, to see it in the first stages of an eclipse and saw the whole procedure. It was a full eclipse and lasted about two hours. Spent the following night on Anjuna beach sleeping under the stars. It was a bit chilly but a bottle of Caju liquor helped us out. We've really become fond of that stuff – only $1 Australian for a 26 ounce bottle. Anjuna is a lovely beach with rocky headlands and deep water, and the usual dozens of palm trees. Stayed until mid-afternoon, then walked back around the cliff-face. Danny was very good and walked most of each way – about two miles over rough high country.

All this time spent at the beach brought out Charley's artistic side. He sculptured wonderful sand-cars with Danny sitting in the driver's seat. Neither of them seemed to tire of this activity, which was repeated every time we went to the beach.

The Caju liquor was a local spirit made from the fruit of the cashew nut. A picture on the bottle showed a large fruit, similar in size and shape to a mango, with a single little cashew nut attached to the bottom. I never discovered if this was truly the way cashew nuts grew, or artistic licence. It seemed an awfully big fruit for such a small nut. The taste was very agreeable and we drank quite a lot of it.

Our visit coincided with the Exposition of St Francis Xavier in the capital Panjim, a once-in-a-decade event which attracted a lot of Catholics. This was where his body had been taken from the church we'd visited in Malacca in Malaysia where he was originally interred, and I was interested to see him in his final resting place. We dutifully lined up with the believers to pay our respects.

> Much like what I'd expected, pretty dry and shrivelled. The Bom Jesus Church is reasonably impressive, but the paintings and statues were a bit amateurish or melodramatic or something.

Predictably, all didn't stay perfect in paradise. Most westerners succumbed to the numerous Indian infectious diseases, and we were no exception. We all came down with very bad colds which lasted much longer than the standard two weeks. I felt lightheaded for days, unable to concentrate on what I was saying or hearing. We had chronic upset stomachs, nothing drastic, but annoying, and public toilets were thin on the ground. Mosquitoes were common and there was no avoiding being bitten, screens being unheard of. I had several bites on my leg which became infected. One day we traipsed around the port of Vasco da Gama as Charley was enquiring about possible jobs on a ship to Europe. Everyone was at lunch for hours and we weren't allowed on to the wharves, something to do with people stowing away. It was stinking hot and my leg was really painful. Luckily one didn't need a prescription in India for virtually every known drug, and I bought some antibiotic ointment over the counter in a chemist shop. Once back home, I bathed my leg in our clay bowl and put on the ointment. The next day, the infection was gone.

Needless to say, Charley didn't find a job on a ship. With unemployment in India in the millions, four months' experience on a prawn trawler in the Gulf of Carpentaria just didn't cut it.

Chapter 13

Well once again Danny and I are on our own. Charley left this morning by boat for Bombay and we've just returned from seeing him off. I don't think Danny quite understands the whole procedure as he ran on ahead as we approached home to see if Charley was there yet. However the gun Charley gave him just before leaving has proved a great distraction, so I hope he's not too upset when he realises the break is for a length of time. My own feelings are mixed, as for the last few days I've felt better about his leaving, but at the moment I'm feeling rather low I must admit.

With Charley gone, it was a time of reflection. I started weighing up my options. One was to stay on in Goa longer until the hot weather started and the European winter ended. Another was to meet up with my old Sydney friend Leonie and her daughter Melanie, who were by now in Nepal. Finishing the overland trip wasn't really an option as travelling for days on buses and trains in the colder weather didn't appeal. Danny was a good traveller but it was close to 6000 kilometres by road and rail between Bombay and Istanbul. I consulted Danny to see how he felt about this simple lifestyle we were now living.

"Hey Danny, would you like to stay here or go back to Adelaide to live?"

He looked concerned. "I can't find Charley in Adelaide," was his conclusion. Somehow he'd picked up that we were all joining up again sometime.

For my part, I wondered where my relationship with Charley was leading. We seemed so compatible, but I had always felt his single-mindedness. If he wanted to do something, he did it. Discussing it as a couple and reaching a decision together just wasn't how he did things. After my two former relationships with dependent, insecure guys, I was initially delighted with Charley's self-sufficiency, but I expected to be included in future planning. I felt a lingering uneasiness. Perhaps my ideal lay somewhere between the two?

The days drifted by much as before. The only difference without Charley around was I went to sleep earlier. I was literally stung into action by the arrival of countless fleas and resorted to the local treatment of sprinkling DDT powder through the bedroom, blankets and clothes. Charley and Danny were mosquito magnets, whereas they largely ignored me. However, whatever it was in me that repelled mosquitoes attracted fleas and I was covered in bites.

A head-lice infestation struck the kindergarten and we all had to wash our hair with a special shampoo which was abundant in the village shops. Little Dolma, sensing my ignorance, showed me how to catch cooties as she called them and squash them between my thumbnails. I thanked her very earnestly for this information, but stuck with the shampoo.

The school closed for Christmas and Danny and I usually spent the mornings in the village, about a kilometre away. En route we stopped at a little roadside stall and had puris and dahl, served on a saucer. Danny wasn't too keen on the dahl but liked the puris, small discs of flat Indian bread. Heavy wooden carts pulled by docile white oxen slowly rolled past as we sat at the roadside table.

This was my first Christmas out of Australia, away from family and friends. We went to a party on Christmas Eve at the nearby Seaview Cottages.

> The bottles of Caju and coconut fenny, glasses of punch, chillums and joints were passing at a mile a minute so before any time had passed

everybody was well on the way. It turned out a very dreamy party – everyone sat on the verandah of the cottages which are right on the beach and went off into their own little world. It was a beautiful moonlit night – almost a three-quarter moon and the palm trees really stood out against the sand.

Later they all rallied and went into the village to midnight mass at the church. I was disappointed I couldn't go as Danny was sound asleep and too heavy to carry. I could have left him home with Anthony's family, but hadn't realised church was on the agenda. Not being Catholic, I'd never been to midnight mass and would have liked to attend an Indian service.

By Australian standards, there wasn't much available in the shops in the way of Christmas presents for small boys, but Danny was engrossed with the double-decker bus, book and two small animals I gave him, and the racing car and doll from Father Christmas. I was a bit dubious about the afternoon Christmas party. We were going to Helen and Ingo's, the parents of Danny's little friend Carlie.

I hope this afternoon's party at Helen's comes off ok and that Ingo isn't as wiped out and as repulsive as usual. I'd leave post haste if I were Helen. It's incredible how he reminds me of

Ken – nag nag nag from the moment he opens his mouth. Helen is incapable of doing a thing right seen through his bloodshot eyes.

Ingo and Helen were regular visitors to Goa. They came once the monsoon ended and stayed for months. I suspected the major attraction for Ingo was the cheap alcohol, not just the caju which Charley and I fancied, but also fenny made from coconuts. He was one of these boring drunks who insisted on holding the floor, but talked rubbish. There was no doubt he had a drinking problem and I felt for Helen, stuck in this situation so far from home. They invariably ran out of money before they wanted to return to Europe and had to resort to sending small quantities of hash oil through the post to contacts in Germany and Britain.

I was also dubious about another probable guest at the party.

I hope in a way that Helge isn't there. Not that he's so bad at all, but he decided to make himself my first "occasional visitor" to use his own words and came bashing on the doors at about 11 pm one night last week and ended up waking Anthony. I pretended to be asleep of course. He wanted me to take a shipment of hash into Australia for $6000 Australian, but I declined, even though I'm sure it's foolproof as the stuff is welded into a sports machine and re-sprayed. After he realised I wouldn't go, he decided to chat about other things and decided what I really needed was this "occasional lover".

I declined that offer as well. I must have been a major disappointment. Helge was another of the European hippies who stayed in Goa for the season and financed his lifestyle by exporting hash. Apparently his previous drug mule had got cold feet on the way to the airport and bailed out. Helge was scathing about this, his anger obvious. He insisted it was foolproof. I wondered in that case why he didn't take it himself, but kept my mouth shut.

"Customs officers wouldn't look twice at an Australian mother and child," he insisted.

I wasn't convinced. If I were an astute customs officer, I might be suspicious of a hippie mother with child in tow, importing a sports machine. A sports machine? From India? Since when did hippies exercise, or India make sports machines? A statue of Buddha maybe...

There were no hard feelings as at the next full-moon party on Anjuna Beach Helge gave me some of his precious cocaine stash. This he kept in a little silver container, to be inhaled from the bowl of a tiny silver spoon. He chided me for spilling some, but in reality his hands were shaking as he held the spoon.

It was dawn and we watched the full moon setting into the sea as the sun rose behind us. The cocaine must have had an effect as I snapped out of my comatose state from being awake most of the night, and started chatting with Helge who told me he used to be a junkie but was cured after taking six tablets of LSD which freaked him out completely.

He also told me about the red VW Kombi he drove which had caused him grief in the past. In India, if you brought in a vehicle from another country, it had to be listed in your passport, engine number and all. This was to stop the owner from selling it while in India, something which wasn't allowed. Perhaps it was to protect the shaky Indian car manufacturing industry. Helge had lent it to a friend while he went off somewhere, but when he came back, the friend plus car were nowhere to be found. This was a major drama as he was to fly out in a day or two, and without the car which was to go into storage while he was away, he would be fined a hefty amount, it being assumed the car had been sold. Helge had no choice but to cough up.

The following year Helge flew back into Panjim. As the plane landed, there was his red Kombi driving along the road into the airport. The friend was confronted and the car reclaimed. Helge took all this in his stride, no doubt accepting the hippie lifestyle had different rules from those back in the real world.

Danny and I took the long way back home from the party to Calangute. The previous day we'd taken the short cut over the headland.

We walked over the hill to Anjuna, got lost and ended up floundering through the undergrowth but made it to the top eventually. Saw a large cobra moving very slowly through the short grass so immediately decided to go home the next day via the coast path.

We followed the snake at a safe distance, until it stopped and raised its head, flaring the skin in typical cobra fashion. I was used to snakes, having been brought up in an area where brown snakes were common, but was well aware that a cobra bite on that deserted hill on the Indian coast would most likely have been a death sentence.

*

In the end, my wavering about future plans was taken out of my hands. I got word that my sister Rosemary was arriving in London in January. She was 17 years old and my mother would only let her go if I was there to keep an eye on her, which I had tentatively agreed to do earlier on. It was time to leave our laid-back world.

A few days later we were in Poona, home of Bhagwan Shree Rajneesh. In Goa, I'd read his magazine, *Sanyassin*, and decided to visit the ashram on our way to Bombay. The day started with active meditation which involved a lot of movement from 6 am to 7 am, a lecture by Bhagwan from 8 am to 9.30 am, and another active meditation in the early evening. The devotees at the ashram were very welcoming and in no time we'd been taken under the wing of a Swiss-American family: grandmother, two daughters, one son-in-law and grandson Siddharta, named after the Buddha and the same age as Danny.

I went to a couple of Bhagwan's talks. He was a charismatic speaker, his spiritual and philosophical topics delivered in an engaging manner, easily understood by his orange-clad loyal subjects. We'd arrived just at the end of the lecture series in English, the following block being in Hindi. One evening I was in a small room with just Bhagwan and a few devotees. Bhagwan sat in an armchair near big windows opening out to the night sky. A young English girl dressed in white who was sitting at Bhagwan's feet, in response to a request from him began what could best be described as a shimmy. Still seated, her face and arms raised towards the darkness, she appeared almost in a trance as the upper part of her body moved rapidly. From where I sat, she was a stark white against the blackness and the effect was mesmerising.

When it was discovered I was on my way to London where they had another ashram, I was laden with books and letters to personally deliver. I had to stand firm and restrict this to a small shoulder bag. My rucksack was so heavy I could barely lift it, and a sleeping three-year-old is no light weight. They reluctantly lightened the load.

Bombay was a city of contrasts. We'd just passed through on our way to Goa, and now had more time to look around. Wide streets, modern buildings, beggars everywhere. Danny loved the bright-red double-decker buses and we spent hours in them riding around the city, on the top deck of course.

We stayed in the Rex Hotel, awaiting our flight to London. Someone had written on the wall in ballpoint pen: *"This room is infested with bed-bugs"* followed by a date from a few months earlier. We didn't have much choice. Budget accommodation was scarce and the previous night we'd stayed at the Miramar.

> Twenty lousy rupees a night for a rickety bed which half collapsed (luckily there was another in the room) and an excuse for a mattress which covers only two thirds of the bed. We had a most uncomfortable night and both kept waking up all the time. Fortunately it wasn't cold. There's no running water anywhere, hot or cold,

and we're given a bucketful to last the day. The time to go to the toilet is first thing in the morning as there's no water to flush them and you can imagine what they're like by the evening. Second rate hotels have long since lost their novelty and I long for a bit of cleanliness, hot running water and pleasant surroundings. I'll never spend any length of time in a depressing place in the future – no matter what the cost.

Famous last words… I think the universe was giving me the message it was high time to leave. It was now January, and I'd left Adelaide the previous March.

As Danny and I settled down for our last night in Asia, I was awoken by a vague discomfort. Was something crawling on my skin? I switched on the light and pulled back the sheet to see tiny psychedelic bugs, some red, others green, scurrying back into the mattress. There were also a few larger ones, light-brown in colour. I checked the backs of my thighs and upper arms and found the tell-tale red bites, softer flesh being favoured by bed bugs. Cursing, I spread my plastic groundsheet on to the cold terrazzo floor, lifted Danny, still sleeping, onto it and counted the hours till daybreak.

Feeling wretched, I got out my pen and wrote on the wall beneath the previous victim's message: *"They're still here 14–1–75."*

Chapter 14

The plane's wheels bumped along the runway at Heathrow. Not a smooth landing.

"Hey Danny, we're in London."

London, mid-winter to be sure, but still London, the yearned-for destination of generations of Australians. I'd made it.

We lined up for Immigration, then Customs, and at last escaped into the Arrivals Lounge, looking for Charley. He'd warned me he could be working at his factory job, but I was ever optimistic. However, it was not to be, and we caught a big black London taxi to Charley's bed-sitter in Sudbury. By now it was pitch dark, our first taste of the short winter days.

I knocked at the darkened door, waited, then knocked again, shivering in my red cotton wrap-around Indian skirt and light cotton top. My Amco blue denim jacket was no match for an English winter. A light came on, then the door opened. Charley's familiar frame filled the doorway.

"I've got the flu," he said by way of greeting, coughing into his handkerchief all the way back up the steps to his room.

Shivering fits overcame him. His single wooden-framed bed bashed against the wall during these attacks. I was dubious about his self-diagnosis and we got a more professional opinion. He spent the next four days in hospital being treated for malaria.

*

I felt like the wheels were falling off. After travelling for so long, all I wanted was some normality, to settle in an ordinary house, do everyday things. Charley, usually so laidback, was irritable, no doubt because of his illness, wavering between anxiety about being evicted because of Danny and me staying with him as he wasn't allowed guests, and being blasé as it was just a bed-sit after all, one of thousands in London. Whenever I said I'd start looking for somewhere else to live, he'd relent and want us to stay. If the situation was reversed, I'd have wanted us to be together. After all, we'd just been apart. The warning bells were ringing.

I feel as if I know Charley pretty well now. He's always trying to get off by himself, which he thinks he prefers, but once alone he feels in need of familiar faces again. His letters always get more intense the longer we've been apart, but as soon as we're together he starts building up the barriers again.

In the end, the situation resolved itself. My sister and her boyfriend were going to Europe for a couple of weeks and I moved into their share-house in Fulham while they were gone. The others in the house were all very friendly, out all day at work which gave Danny and me the run of the place. Only one, Joe, was there through the day, but asleep as he worked nights. Danny and I fed the pigeons in Trafalgar Square and wandered down Whitehall past Downing Street to Big Ben. All the familiar places of an Anglo-Australian education were coming to light.

I put an ad in *Time Out* magazine. This was *the* magazine for young people – the bands to see, the pubs to drink in, the in-places to live: *Single mother with young son seeks shared accommodation. Happy to live with others in similar situation.*

I knew nothing of the London rental accommodation scene. Back in Sydney it was easy. You found a house with several bedrooms and advertised for housemates. However, large houses didn't exist in

London. Everything had been sub-divided into flats and bedsits. I had a few calls from people with a spare room to rent, but I needed to live with other single parents so we could share childcare. Then I hit the jackpot. I had a call from a young English woman called Pam.

> On Thursday I found us a really nice flat – bedroom, lounge, kitchen, bathroom, toilet. Nice and modern in a big three-storey house with a big yard in Putney. The house itself is old and impressive-looking and has been divided into several flats. It only costs ten pounds a week as the girl whose husband owns it (they're separated) wants someone to share baby-sitting as she has a four-year-old son. She's really nice, swinging and 30 years old.

Pam was tall, slim, gorgeous-looking and chatty. She and her son lived in the flat next door. Perfect.

*

If Charley had continued his malaria medication for the recommended two weeks after leaving India, he wouldn't have caught malaria. If he hadn't caught malaria, he wouldn't have lost his factory job. If he hadn't lost his factory job, he wouldn't have applied for a job as a deck-hand in the Mediterranean he saw in a London newspaper. If he hadn't applied for that job, he wouldn't have got it, and he would have stayed in London as planned.

The best-laid plans of mice and men... I felt powers beyond me were taking over my life, someone else was at the steering wheel. But despite Charley's imminent departure, we made the best of our time left together.

> Charley and I had a great touristy day last Sunday. Jane from the Fulham flat minded Danny and we went to Speakers Corner in Hyde Park, through St James' Park to Buckingham Palace, then to Westminster Cathedral, Westminster Bridge and the Houses of Parliament. All in a very compact area – most obliging of them. We had a very good day and were looking forward to a few more, moan, moan. We had a farewell dinner in an Italian restaurant in Earl's Court Road on Friday night. I didn't let his approaching departure spoil things, and we really had a good time.

Charley left a few days after Danny and I moved into our new home. I felt desolate. We'd reached our destination after nearly a year on the road. Now what? We didn't have to wait long to find out. Life continued to get in the way of my happiness.

Surviving the Seventies

*

Danny and I had been there a week when I heard a noise at the door. Someone was breaking in. I yanked the door open to be confronted by a very surprised, very apologetic tradesman. He had no idea anyone was living here – he had instructions from the property's owner to gain access to all the flats. It turned out that Pam shouldn't have been there at all; she'd taken advantage of her knowledge of the unoccupied property to move herself in, and had sub-let to me illegally. When she came home, she told me we'd both have to leave – the place had been sold. Her ex-husband would pay me back my £40 bond, which she'd spent. Peter her ex duly turned up and forked out the money. He was very good-looking and charming – no doubt hoping not to have any trouble from me as evicting tenants was a very difficult and costly business in the UK in those days. We moved back to my sister's place in Fulham.

Despite the fact that Pam and I had only just met and the subsequent mess I found myself in, she and I stayed in touch and continued to write for a couple of years. Perhaps we recognised kindred spirits.

25th Feb: I'm having a bad day again today. I feel low and depressed and that the future in London holds nothing for me. At such times as this friends are what you need, and they're all miles away. I'm very lucky to be here in Fulham as Joe and Dave have taken it upon themselves to cheer me up and took me to the Leinster last Sunday night. We had a ball surprisingly enough and Joe and I staggered home arm in arm, holding each other up. It's a shame he's not a bit taller...

Perhaps I wasn't destined to be the faithful stay-at-home type?

I was back flat-hunting again. Agents wouldn't look at an unemployed single mother and child, and being Australian made it worse. I had plenty of money to pay for bond and rent, but English law back in the seventies favoured the tenant. Once in, it took six months through the courts to evict a dud renter. In an attempt to guard tenants from exploitative landlords the law makers hadn't foreseen how this could exclude ordinary people like me, the very people they were trying to protect.

Chapter 15

Once again fate stepped in. Joe from the Fulham flat was from Ireland and worked as a house-painter on contract with an Irish company. He had holidays coming up and asked if I wanted to go to Ibiza in Spain with him. He'd been there before and loved it. Although I was well and truly over travelling, this seemed like a good way out of my London hassles. I'd already planned to visit Charley at some stage in Antibes in the south of France where his boat was based, and a glance at the map of Europe showed me that Spain and France bordered each other.

Joe, Danny and I boarded the bus from London late one dark afternoon. We crossed the Pyrenees in the middle of the night and arrived in Barcelona the next day in time to get the evening boat across to

Ibiza. The sea was calm but with a big swell. We woke early the next morning, had a sweet plain bun each for breakfast, and in no time were throwing up over the rail. Thank God it was only a couple of hours till we docked.

The trip didn't work out so well. Joe and I had very little to talk about. He was five years younger than me, away from his Irish village home for the first time. He told me his mother and sisters had stood at the front gate crying when he left for London. To make matters worse, the weather was terrible for most of the eight days we were together. Joe was disappointed as the previous time he'd been there it was the height of the holiday season, and now it was very quiet. However, Ibiza itself appealed to me. I must have still been in my rustic hippie persona – you could rent a farmhouse for £24 a month. I toyed with the idea of coming back to live after visiting Charley in France. The only hitch was that one needed a vehicle, public transport being sparse.

Joe was off to Morocco in a van with a group of travellers we'd met on Ibiza. I was glad for him, sure he'd have a more exciting time than we'd had together. Danny and I caught the ferry back to Barcelona, careful not to eat anything this time, and had a day in the city before crossing the border.

We saw Columbus's column, his flagship the Santa Maria, the Picasso Art Gallery and the church of the Sagrada Familia which I thought hideous. We climbed thousands of steps to the top of the towers, but the view of Barcelona was restricted by the lousy architecture.

This church is considered Gaudi's masterpiece – perhaps I needed to do an architecture appreciation course. Or maybe I was just exhausted from dragging Danny up the stairs.

To get to Antibes from Barcelona involved three different trains. We almost missed our connection in Marseilles as it was 3 am and I was sound asleep. The Mediterranean coast was like the postcards – blue sea and skies, castles and ruins. Antibes had its own fortress, high on the cliffs overlooking the sea.

We found our way to the port. I spoke to the harbour master in my best schoolgirl French: "Bonjour Monsieur, où est le *Zulu Charlie*?"

The *Zulu Charlie* was Charley's motor yacht, named by its new American owner after the call sign of the plane he flew during World War Two, changing it from the *Mary Fisher* which I preferred. However the yacht was out on manoeuvres and wouldn't be back till the next day. For the third time I'd rocked up somewhere to meet Charley, only to find him not there. This was getting to be a habit.

A week or so later Charley, Danny and I were sharing a two-bedroomed flat with Robin, the first mate on the *Zulu Charlie* and his girlfriend, Pauline, who had also just arrived from London. We were very lucky to find the flat as even though it wasn't yet April the holiday season was approaching and most rental accommodation had long gone.

In the local playground I met a young French woman who'd lived in the US and Australia, and now was back in her home in the old section of Antibes, right on the sea wall. She had a little girl Danny's age and guided me around the local kindergartens. But regulations were strict in France. Enrolment was only in September, the start of the school year. No exceptions.

In London I'd had job prospects, a kindergarten but nowhere to live. In Antibes I had a great place to live, job prospects but no kindergarten.

We soon fell into a routine. We were all up at 6.30, even Danny, for Charley and Robin's early start. Danny and I spent a lot of time at the playground with my new French friend, her little daughter, an Australian au pair Janet and her young charge, Bradley. After a session at the swings we'd go off to coffee together. Janet had committed herself back in Australia to travelling with an Australian doctor and his family for six months. It sounded good on paper: au pair for a wealthy family on the Grand Tour of Europe, all expenses paid.

I asked her how it was going. Working as an au pair was a popular way of seeing Europe, but usually jobs were found with a local family through an agency in London, not back home with an Australian family.

"It's been rather beaut, actually," Janet answered. I can still remember her comment, struck by both the ockerish Australian and her obvious insincerity.

Janet had been flattered when she was chosen, but didn't think it through. In reality, she was in a strange place with only a three-year-old boy for company all day, five days a week. Meeting the locals was unlikely as she only spoke basic French and in the evenings she was stuck in rental accommodation with her employers. If she'd been working for a French family, she would have met their extended family and circle of friends and learned the language. If she went out at night, there were limited places to go as a single woman. Antibes didn't have the British pub scene and going into a French bar alone would have felt very uncomfortable. The doctor gave her a generous amount each day to entertain Bradley but Janet comforted herself with French pastries and the weight was piling on. Our flat was a haven for her and she escaped there whenever she could, desperate to relate to anyone who wasn't three or French.

Janet was from a large family in Melbourne and had expected to be made to feel at home in her new job, but in reality the wife treated her like a servant, with disdain. She even got her doing housework, which wasn't part of the deal.

"She's a real pill," Janet said. I laughed. I hadn't heard that term in years.

I met her employers on a few occasions and had to agree with Janet. The doctor was warm and friendly, his wife a snob. Janet was counting the days till her departure date.

"Why don't you leave?" I asked.

"Oh, I made a commitment back in Melbourne, I'd feel bad about leaving early."

The work ethic was deeply entrenched in the Australian working class back then. They were due to move on to Greece soon for a month or so. I hoped the new environment would at least be a distraction for a while.

Charley and Robin worked 12-hour plus days on the boat now undergoing a refit, which was interesting for Charley who previously couldn't hammer a nail. He chatted on easily about his day on the boat. My day in the playground didn't add much to the conversation. I was turning into a Desperate Housewife.

To break the routine, we'd go sightseeing.

Another sunny afternoon in Antibes! The weather certainly is lovely when the sun shines and the Mistral isn't blowing. Last Sunday Janet, Danny and I went to St Paul, a little village inland from the coast. Had a wander round the Foundation Maeght, a modern art gallery set in lovely gardens. The village itself is still largely in its original form, with the ramparts still almost all intact. Little winding streets and narrow archways – probably typical of French villages in this area. The village church was somewhat cluttered I thought with many altars and paintings, not as nice as the church here in Antibes, which was full of flowers when we saw it at Easter.

On Friday I hope to be the owner of a VW van of doubtful age but reasonable condition, for 2000 francs (£200). If only my money would arrive. It's two months now since I arranged to have it sent through the Bank of NSW in Sackville Street. I take back all I said about Asian incompetence. Two months to send £300 from Australia to London! I've given up on them and written to mum to send it here direct.

Pauline and I also made a bit of money by doing the *Zulu Charlie*'s laundry, only charging half the commercial rate, but our fee was still extortionate. Janet offered her "family's" wash as well, giving us what she'd have spent at the laundry. Things were looking up. The little washing machine in our flat laboured with all the sheets etc from the boat, and was inclined to break down. It was my job to ring the landlord to complain as Pauline couldn't speak any French at all. However, after a few episodes of "*De nouveau, la machine ne fonctionne plus*", he lost his cool and blasted me in French over the phone.

Just as well it was nearly time to leave Antibes.

I was getting in a fouler mood as each day passed. I had no money. Charley was supporting us all from his meagre wage, I'd paid the deposit on the VW van which was sitting on the wharf waiting for the balance, and the *Zulu Charlie* was due to leave in nine days. What would I do then?

My request for £300 had vaporised somewhere between the UK and South Australia during the last two months. My mother had gone to the head office in Adelaide to arrange the transfer herself and had written to tell me the money was on its way, but omitted the name of the bank in Cannes. How many banks were there in Cannes? I didn't trust the British boat captain who owned the Kombi not to sell it if he got another offer. He struck me as a wheeler and dealer.

But somehow I found the bank, paid off my debts and drove around Antibes in my new green Kombi. It was a right-hand drive, originally British, but here had to be driven on the right. Being 25, it never occurred to me this might be tricky, and it wasn't. Charley leaped behind the wheel, not having driven a vehicle for over a year, and roared off down the wharf, scraping the side along a wall. He later broke off the only key in the driver's door lock, impatient as it was a bit stiff, leaving me to start the car with my nail scissors in the ignition. Some things never change, the behaviour of young guys being one of them.

I found a locksmith in Cannes and presented the broken pieces. He did his best to copy them but the new key wouldn't open the door. He declared there was a piece missing. I didn't blame him for the failure of the new key – after all the old one was in fragments – but I knew there were no more pieces, and said so. He went off his trolley at me, in French of course. Sometimes French behaviour floored me. Perhaps he thought I wasn't going to pay?

On another occasion I'd taken my cassette player to an electronics place to have it repaired. A little wire had broken off. I'd seen it break and told the guy in the shop where to solder it back on, but afterwards when I tried to play it, it didn't work.

"*Ce doit être autre chose*," I said philosophically.

However the shopkeeper started yelling at me, something about my husband working on the boats was all I understood. I stood there dumbstruck. I didn't blame him for the player not working and I intended to pay for his labour. My husband's job didn't come into it. Later back home when I examined the soldering job more closely I saw he hadn't done it properly and had actually missed the little silver contact I'd pointed out to him.

I set out for another locksmith, but somehow found myself on the motorway. My simmering fury with Charley boiled over and I yelled obscenities at the top of my voice through the open window as we roared back along the 12 kilometres to Antibes, unable to escape.

But I soon put these calamities behind me. Now I had wheels. I was in control.

Last Sunday, we three set off for the snow. At last! Drove through Isola and Auron to St Étienne de Tinée where Charley and I had a lovely meal which unfortunately we couldn't eat very much of as we both felt really full after the entree. Spent the night there, then drove back to the snowfields at Auron and passed a couple of hours throwing snowballs at each other. Drove up to St Dalmas de Selvage and went for a walk through the snow. It was lovely, not even too cold. Returned via Beuil and the Gorges du Cians – the most unusual red-rock formations I have ever seen.

Coming from the driest state in the driest continent, this was only the third time I'd seen snow. It was Danny's second as we had spent a June long weekend back in NSW at the opening of the ski season, inspecting the occasional melting patch mixed with mud among the gum trees in the Snowy Mountains.

I may be the only person ever to have driven from the south of France to Paris using nail scissors as an ignition key, but didn't give it a second thought. The van couldn't be properly locked anyway as the catch on one of the little side windows was broken. The former owner Fred had made a half-hearted effort to wire it closed. I had nothing worth stealing. My sister Rosemary and her boyfriend Mark were coming to Paris on their way to Morocco, bringing some of my stuff I'd left in London. It was a good excuse to take the new car for a run. Enforced inactivity in Antibes was beginning to pall. Danny and I left Antibes on May 6th and headed into the mountains. It never crossed my mind that driving an old Kombi up narrow winding roads into the Alps in the pouring rain might be a problem, and it wasn't.

We camped overnight in a town called Gap.

Set out early on the 8th for Grenoble and wended our way higher and higher into the Haute-Alpes, surrounded by snow and cloud-covered mountains. The colour of the rocks is very spectacular and changes every few miles. If I didn't know it was spring, I'd be sure it was autumn as the trees and foliage are every shade imaginable. The weather was much kinder and the sun actually shone once or twice.

Perhaps it was the extreme contrast with Australia, but France struck me as such a pretty place – little villages, churches, spires, ruins of castles, Roman ruins, little farms in the green, gold, brown and russet countryside.

We passed the perfect village – La Rochepot, north of Chalon-sur-Saône. On the side of a hill little red-roofed houses clustered together, surrounded by greenery. Surveying it all above the village was the most incredible castle with huge conical-shaped metallic structures where the roofs should be. I was most annoyed at having just used my last photograph in Lyon.

I had plenty of maps – the last person to drive this Kombi around Europe had left a big box full – but no tourist guidebook. I was struck by how many brilliant places I'd come across by accident, by merely driving on a direct route up through France to Paris, taking the backroads. I wrote a list of the towns and villages we had to pass through and put it in front of me on the dashboard. I met an Australian couple in their fifties in one of the campsites en route who couldn't believe I hadn't got lost – they said they were, constantly. I have no sense of direction so my simple little list must have worked.

On the third day we arrived in Paris and by some miracle drove through the centre of the city, past the Arc de Triomphe straight to the campsite at the Bois de Boulogne where we were to meet my sister. The place was huge. After wandering through enough tents to form a military encampment we gave up and settled in for the night. Camping is a very popular French way of holidaying. We woke early and continued our search but it was mid-morning before we found each other.

This was turning into a Claytons Grand Tour of Europe – the grand tour you have when you're not having a tour. Circumstances had so far taken me to Spain, the South of France and now up through the country to Paris to meet my sister and her boyfriend. And all I had wanted was to stay in London.

We spent a few days being tourists. Mark had been to Paris before and I sensed his impatience to get on the road to their destination, Morocco. We lost Danny while crushed in the crowd trying to see the Mona

Lisa at the Louvre. We split up to find him. Mark came across him 20 minutes later, wandering along a corridor, just starting to whimper as it dawned on him he was all alone. Visions of French perverts had taken the edge off our visit, and we left.

We wandered through the lakes and trees of the Bois de Boulogne and came across a show-jumping competition in progress, in an area adjoining the woods. Mindful of our tight budget, we climbed over the back fence and sat amongst the impeccably dressed French, our shabby jeans and T-shirts drawing disapproving stares.

Not far from the campsite, I discovered Auto Clé and soon had two new keys for the car.

Charley was finally forgiven. I sadly dropped my nail-scissors into a rubbish bin, their temporary life as an ignition key having rendered them useless at cutting anything. We headed south, back to Antibes. Once again it was a smorgasbord of sights, even if one wasn't really sightseeing. We visited the palace of Versailles, the cathedral at Chartres and found ourselves amongst the chateaus of the Loire Valley. My favourite was Chenonceau, Catherine de Medici's home, with its huge grounds and a river which ran beneath parts of the castle.

The countryside around Bourges and south was beautiful – fields of yellow mustard weed and yellow and white daisies. Would have loved to see Aily-le-vieil, but sensed that Mark was in a hurry to get where we were going.

I was starting to see a side of Mark I hadn't been aware of in London. He was very controlling and critical, putting my sister down in front of others. He reminded me of Ken, Danny's father. Rosemary had contracted a urinary tract infection in Paris, and we found a doctor along the way as she wasn't improving. I explained her symptoms in my schoolgirl French and soon had antibiotics and a big bottle of a disinfectant solution.

"There goes your birthday present," said Mark when he saw the bill. She'd just turned 18 and he was going to buy her a pendant as a gift. I kept my mouth shut, not interfering with the business of others being firmly entrenched.

She eventually dumped him via a letter sent to Singapore when he was on his way home, intending to join her back in Adelaide. I was delighted with her decision, and this time didn't keep my opinion to myself.

By now we were in the Massif Central, accurately named as it was in the middle of the country and very mountainous. The town of Le Puy-en-Velay stood out, literally, with a colossal red cast-iron statue of the Madonna perched on top of a towering pinnacle of volcanic rock. You could climb up inside the Madonna, which we did but I thought it rather weird, somewhat sacrilegious.

South again through the Rhone Valley, the Roman presence everywhere.

> Spent the night outside Nîmes, and the following morning wandering round the Arena, Maison Carrée and the Temple of Diana, set in landscaped gardens and Roman waterways. The weather was beautiful and sunny – a really lovely place.

At last we were back at the Mediterranean. Mark wanted to have a look at St Tropez, unimpressive as the weather was dull. I can't hear St Tropez mentioned without thinking of a tale a friend told me years later. He was in the London Underground waiting for a train, idly looking at the huge advertising billboards lining the tunnel. One for Smirnoff Vodka caught his eye. A nubile young girl dressed in a bikini, designer sunglasses perched on the tip of her nose, languishes in a deckchair on a sunny beach overlooking a sparkling deep blue sea. She is sipping from a long frosty glass replete with ice-cubes, slice of lemon and bright pink straw.

The caption read: "I thought St Tropez was a Trappist monk until I tasted Smirnoff."

Some wag had graffitied below in large letters: "I thought Wan-king was the capital of China until I tasted Smirnoff."

Twenty years later I still have to laugh whenever I come across a reference to St Tropez or Smirnoff.

*

Antibes at last! Back home! And the *Zulu Charlie* was still in port.

Danny and I were now living in the van. We'd given up the flat as the yacht had been due to leave for the Greek Islands while I was in Paris, but yet another delay kept it moored in Antibes. Charley didn't join us until eight o'clock, after dinner on board. This enforced inactivity was driving me mad. I'd always led such a busy life. As a kid there were never enough hours in the day. I went straight into full-time work and part-time study after high school, then single parenthood during my final year of training in the laboratory. My life had been work, caring for Danny, house-sharing and raging around Sydney's night spots. Lack of sleep became the norm. Even travelling in Asia had been a full-time occupation. I didn't know how to handle idleness.

Chapter 16

I lasted a couple of weeks then headed for Rome to meet my brother Bruce who was flying in from Hong Kong. A flat tyre, broken accelerator cable and an electrical fault kept us in the campground in Pisa for four days.

> There are countless New Zealand, Australian and Great Britain Kombis here. We're part of the Great Commonwealth Kombi Scene which appeals not at all. I didn't mind being surrounded by Australians in Asia but it seems stereotyped here. You buy your Kombi, stick on a map, flag and/or kangaroo and "do" Europe. Really revolting! They're great people though, most friendly and funny. I've hardly seen Danny. He's always off playing with the "big boys".

The day I left Antibes, after a couple of hours heading towards Italy, I turned around and headed towards England, then turned round and headed back through Italy. I was in tears. I didn't want this nomadic life any more, but didn't want to be apart from Charley. My restlessness clashed with his utter dedication to his job and our relationship was suffering, but I felt pretty sure if I took myself back to the UK for six months while Charley was in the Mediterranean, our relationship wouldn't last.

In Florence we stayed in a campground near the Piazzalle Michelangelo, which is a lookout across the River Arno and the city. Kon-Tiki buses rolled in regularly and deposited their loads of young Antipodeans doing Europe.

> God the people here are dreadful! Talk about a concentration of ockers. I've decided that applies to New Zealanders as well. There are countless tourist coaches filled with homely Australian girls out-numbering the guys ten to one, and thoroughly miserable about it.
>
> I'm sure it's not because I'm jaded now I've been on the road for ages. The people I met in Asia were my type of people. These aren't. It's as simple as that. I haven't met a soul I've felt an affinity for, and I haven't been overly antisocial.

These coach trips seemed to be one long noisy drinking binge. I wondered what the locals thought of young Australians and New Zealanders. However, they couldn't all have been that bad...

Spent the first day sightseeing with Robyn, Gay and Bruce, three Australians we met here. Wandered round the Duomo and Baptistery which is supposed to have fabulous "Door of Paradise" carvings but I wasn't particularly impressed. Went to the Uzzi Galleries – the usual paintings and sculptures. The Ponte Vecchio is most unusual – houses on the side of a bridge. A group of us went marketing on Wednesday – leather and denim abound but not so cheap I thought. I replaced my Nepalese purse with a similar one in leather – the extent of my Florence souvenirs. Had lunch in a restaurant – huge pizzas.

Danny and I wandered around the Pitti Palace and gardens. I loved the gardens. They stretch for acres with mazes of hedges hiding countless sculptures. Not particularly well attended which I liked – and tending to be overgrown.

My opinion of my fellow countrymen hadn't mellowed by the time we got to Rome.

We're in the Seven Hills camping site, about 11 km north west of Rome. It's a beautiful site, lots of trees, and coachloads of dreadful Australians. Dreadful! Actually saw yoked oxen on the way here – like Asia all over again. Wild flowers were everywhere and in the fields of wheat there were almost as many red poppies as wheat. I've got a cut on my foot which is bleeding a bit – Danny just came and squeezed my foot and said it was getting flatter!

But perhaps my prejudices towards tourists were showing. In Asia, real travellers never took the commercial bus trips across Asia – we looked down on them as soft. Real travellers always caught public transport like the locals. These convoys of coaches roaring across Europe were for wimps.

Rome was full of distractions while we waited for my brother.

Danny and I have seen most of the sights now. The Trevi fountain of "Three Coins in a Fountain" fame, the Capitol (plus its two museums), wandered round the Roman Forum where Caesar was burned and Marc Antony's head displayed. Also the Colosseum and Arch of Constantine. On Sunday we went in the pouring rain to the Vatican City and saw the Pope (briefly) and St Peters with the statue of the Pieta by Michelangelo.

The whole square was jam-packed. When Pope Paul VI appeared on the balcony, the crowd of adoring Catholics surged forward and we were caught in the crush and carried along with it. I fought my way towards a pillar and dragged Danny behind it. We escaped the worst of it, but it was still scary. I've been wary of big crowds ever since.

> Made our way out along the Appian Way to the Catacombs of St Sebastian (he was a Roman turned Christian, and executed by a firing squad of archers – not very nice) The bodies of the Christian martyrs were buried there and during times of oppression it is believed the martyrs themselves used to hide out there. The Catacombs extend to about seven miles into the hills and it is believed the bodies of St Peter and St Paul were, or are, buried there.

After a week or so my brother arrived. We hadn't seen much of each other for a few years. I'd left Adelaide for Sydney, Bruce had been working for the Postmaster-General's Department in the Northern Territory, installing the new microwave system. The last time we'd met had been two years before at my father's hospital bedside, just before he died. While I'd languished on a beach in Goa the previous year, Bruce had survived Cyclone Tracy in Darwin. He told me he'd woken up in the early hours of Christmas morning to the sound of the storm but had gone back to sleep. PMG accommodation was better built than most. The next day he couldn't believe the destruction, his block of flats standing among the ruins. A life-changing experience for him as his job there disappeared in the chaos. He was very laidback – even a battery fire inside the car engine didn't faze him. While I jumped up and down and yelled, he sauntered up with a bottle of water and poured it on the flames.

We headed south for the port of Brindisi to catch the ferry to Greece.

The countryside between Rome and here is all very similar to Australia. No wonder the Italians feel at home there. I'm feeling rather anti-Italian at the moment, having been ripped off everywhere since leaving Rome. A 600 lire meal in a small fishing village ended up costing us a fortune, as the owner kept bringing us little extras which it turned out were not in the meal we ordered. I suppose we should have argued but sometimes it's just too much effort. Then this afternoon we got some petrol and the guy switched the price over before Bruce could check it – 15,500 lire for a tank plus distilled water for the battery. The most I've ever paid before for a full tank is 13,000. The turds! I'll really watch them in future.

On Mt Vesuvius a guide presented Danny with an egg cooked in one of the steaming vents. In nearby Pompeii, I stared with macabre fascination at the casts of a group of people and a dog forever locked into that day in 79 AD. I could still remember the lesson in primary school where I first heard about Pompeii. It had been on my list ever since.

On the day we arrived in the port of Brindisi, I drove from 9 am to 7.30 pm with minimal breaks. Although he planned to join his sister and nephew on a drive through Italy in her Kombi, Bruce hadn't thought to get himself an International Driving Licence. Maybe my mother was to blame, having brought up her family to think women were responsible for everything...

Just saw a final glimpse of Corfu as we steamed out on a very misty day. We had a most pleasant three days there, driving all over the island and swimming, fishing and snorkelling. It's a beautiful place with lots of lovely beaches and calm seas a deep blue – just like the Mediterranean in Antibes. Very primitive in the less-inhabited parts – lots of peasants dressed in black, riding side-saddle on donkeys. They load the donkeys with almost as much as they do in India.

I felt really sad when we berthed on the Georgios, the boat we caught from Brindisi. The whole place was so much like arriving in Panjim in Goa – a similar ship, similar place, same time of day. I really felt Charley's absence strongly, but realised that even if he had stayed in London he could never have afforded to see any of Europe this summer.

We were paddling at one of the beaches, Sidari, when Danny started screaming. Through the clear blue water I could see an octopus with tentacles a foot long, some wrapped around Danny's right ankle, the rest anchored to a rock. I pulled Danny by the arm, the octopus pulled back, Danny yelled and my brother roared with laughter. It wasn't going to let go. Eventually Bruce came and extracted Danny. I was amazed at the creature's strength and determination, but perhaps a chubby white ankle was too much of a temptation.

Some years later I read Gerald Durrell's *My Family and Other Animals* set in Corfu in the last half of the 1930s. Danny's experience with the octopus paralleled his escapades living there as a young boy.

The *Adonis* deposited us at Patras, a port on the north coast of the Peloponnese Peninsula.

Headed south-west of Patras around the coast (sort of). Didn't see too much of the ocean. Then headed inland at Pyrgos to Olympia, the site of the ancient Olympic Games. Jan and Tim who we met on the ship were still with us and we wandered round the ruins for a while. It rained a lot after leaving Olympia which was a pity as the countryside was very mountainous and green. We must have been very high up as we drove through clouds on occasion.

Stopped at a little seaside town called Myli and had several bottles of Retsina, the local rough wine. Got rather boozed, and tried the local kebabs, called souvlaki. Stayed until almost midnight and were descended upon by about a dozen busloads of tourists. Still don't know what the big attraction was. Headed out of town a bit to find a place to camp and ended up in a ditch with the front wheels in the air. Most embarrassing! I was reversing into a cross-road and missed the road I was backing into and landed in the ditch. About 20 Greeks stopped to help and push, and in about 30 minutes or so off we went again. Very friendly people. Parked in a field near a creek and had a chorus of frogs to sleep with.

Went swimming in the sea next morning which was a nice change after the previous day's rain. Set off again for Mycenae and wandered round the ruins there – one of the most important archaeological sites in Greece so we were told. Sort of mediocre, I thought.

Left the Peloponnese Peninsula and drove through dry, barren countryside to Piraeus, Athens' port, where we dropped Jan and Tim off, had a quick look for the *Zulu Charlie*, then found the campsite at Voula, about 20 km south of Athens. Right on the beach.

We spent the whole summer in Greece. My brother left for London soon after we arrived in Athens – no doubt travelling with your sister and nephew was too tame for a 24-year-old guy. Swinging London was calling. Danny cried when he left. Bruce had always been good with kids.

My old friend from Sydney days, Leonie, turned up at last with her daughter Melanie, having followed us across Asia. It was well over a year since we'd last seen each other, when Danny and I left Sydney. We decided to settle in Athens and got a flat in Glyfada, about 20 minutes' drive down the coast.

Charley came and went, depending on the *Zulu Charlie*'s schedule. I found it hard to adjust to being constantly separated. One minute I'd feel happy to see him again, the next distant and unable to relate. I'd been taking the pill for a few months now – sometimes I wondered if it contributed to my mood swings. But by now I'd accepted Charley would always do what he wanted, without discussing plans with me. If I wanted the relationship to continue, I'd have to accept long separations. That wasn't my idea of a relationship and I found myself often thinking of breaking it off. If only he wasn't so appealing...

Leonie and I started working in Bobby's Bar in Piraeus. Compared with Australian wages, we were paid a pittance, but we both wanted to work and it was the best way to become part of the local scene. Bobby was the Greek owner of the bar, which catered mostly to the US servicemen on the nearby bases. He was about 50 with a big black moustache and looked like a Mexican bandit. The Americans were nearly all black, laidback and into raging. When the late shift finished at the bar, we'd all head off to the Cave, a disco set up by a few of the air-force guys. After drinking and dancing until 3 am, they'd go home for a few hours' sleep, then go off to work the next day, bright-eyed and grinning. They were fabulous dancers, African rhythm in their genes. I'd spent the last year listening to *Dark Side of the Moon* and Bob Dylan on my little cassette player. Now we danced to a very different beat, black music. I can still see the black guys in the dimly lit Cave, dancing in unison to "The Bump", bending their knees to bump each other's backsides to the jaunty rhythm.

The British and Australian girls working at the bar were soon hanging around with the black servicemen, Leonie and I included. The white guys didn't bother coming to the bar – they didn't stand a chance. I was intrigued at how muscular the black guys were – most of them didn't do much exercise so that must have been in the genes as well.

> The Negroes have a culture all of their own. Their language is so different, even their handshakes are much different from ours. "Be cool" or "Be sweet" instead of "Goodbye", "What's happening?" instead of "How's things?" "I'm walkin' on the ground, man" when things are low. Funny guys. Once you take everything they say with a pinch of salt, you're halfway there.

I've been going out with Royce Davis, a black guy who's good fun and fabulous in bed. I don't have any guilty feelings about cheating on Charley – it was his idea to work on the bloody yacht. Royce is very self-confident and self-opinionated but rather sweet anyway. He's not well-liked by the other guys as he has a reputation for swiping their girlfriends. We don't have an awful lot to talk about so I guess it's just as well Charley is coming home soon.

Royce was also married – his wife had been in Greece with him but had left him and gone back to the US. "She said she might as well go home because she didn't see anything of me here," he told me. Royce didn't strike me as husband material and I assumed he'd got married very young.

"Is your wife black or white?" I asked. Royce grinned at my naivety.

"She's black," he answered. Black men didn't marry white girls back in the United States of the seventies. Like most Australians from the city, I'd never met an Aborigine, let alone a black American. Although relationships between the girls at the bar and the blacks formed easily, nothing serious ever eventuated. A few of the girls were genuinely besotted with their guys, but a barrier existed. Perhaps the prejudice against mixed race relationships was so firmly ingrained they couldn't contemplate returning to America with a white wife.

Gaye from England was going out with Teddy. They'd planned a night out in Athens. Teddy was getting a new suit made at a local tailor's.

"Will your suit be ready for Saturday?" Gaye asked.

"No, it'll take a few more days," Teddy answered, despondent.

"I was so relieved," Gaye told Leonie and me later. "It's white with lace on the cuffs."

Leonie and I cracked up laughing. The black guys loved outrageous clothes and could get away with it, but apparently this outfit was a step too far.

And just as well I wasn't suffering angst about Charley – I found out later he was having a fling with the cabin girl when they were at sea…

However the universe was against this little dalliance with Royce. The day after Charley left on his last charter for the season, Royce piled his Porsche up against a light pole on King George Highway at 90 miles per hour. He actually got out with hardly a scratch, just a little internal bleeding. The car, Royce's pride and joy, was a write-off. He told me he'd been driving along in his lane when another vehicle pulled on to the highway from a side road, intent on crossing all the lanes to an exit on the other side. He hadn't even seen Royce who had to take evasive action up on to the median strip.

"I said, 'Goodbye Royce' when I saw the pole," he told me.

The medicos wanted to operate to find the source of his internal bleeding. Royce, an operating theatre nurse in real life, refused.

I visited Royce whenever I could. We got chatting about Donna who lived in our block of flats, the wife of a white sailor.

"The difference is that Donna's got no class." Royce's black fingers intertwined with mine.

He lay stretched out in his hospital bed, slowly and painfully changing position every so often. We were talking about Donna's latest exploits. A few weeks back she had been out on the town with friends, eating and drinking in the various bars in Glyfada. She'd drunk a lot, which was her habit, and had woken in the middle of the night in a hotel room, naked, in a double bed between two strange men. She screamed so loudly they threw her, clothes and bag and all, into the corridor.

Donna was now in a state of panic. She confided in me and Leonie that her period was three weeks overdue and she and her husband were soon to be transferred to Italy. If she was pregnant, the baby couldn't be her husband's – he'd been at sea too long. She'd been compos enough on the night of the ménage-à-trois to remember her bed-mates were white. But like most of the ex-pat women we knew, Donna also had a black boyfriend. What if the baby was his?

Leonie and I tried to offer advice. In Greece, it was possible to get terminations, but in Roman Catholic Italy? Donna and her little son BJ flew out of our lives. In the conservative culture of the United States Forces in the seventies her future hung in the balance.

*

It was always hot in Athens. Being raised in Adelaide, I was used to the Mediterranean climate, but in an Adelaide summer there'd be a heatwave for a few days followed by a cool change, another heatwave and so on until summer ended. Some summers were cool and didn't have a day over the old century.

But in Athens, it never cooled down. Once the heat started in June, it stayed hot until October. There was never a cool change. Even sightseeing at the Acropolis was an effort – all those steps to climb up while the hot, dry, dusty wind never stopped blowing. We started eating like the locals – shasliks of lamb or calamari, Greek salads, plain yoghurt which was sold in big pottery bowls, honeydew melon and watermelon. Because of the heat, stodgy food didn't appeal at all. Leonie and I, having spent half our life in Sydney dieting, now started losing weight without effort. Always working through a meal break also helped although Bobby let the staff drink as much as they liked while they worked, which didn't help the diet or efficiency. One day Bobby came to the tables outside the bar brandishing a near-empty bottle of Scotch. He bailed up our workmate Gaye, waving the bottle in her face and telling her off as she'd drunk most of it herself while working the previous night. She apologised calmly, not easy to do confronted with Bobby's aggression, black eyes, black hair, black moustache in her face... I disliked Bobby, he reminded me too much of Danny's father, Ken.

There was even an American forces radio station, which came as no surprise. One day I was home in the flat listening to their DJ playing the latest rock music when the session finished and a woman's soft voice announced the cooking segment, which was an eggplant dish recipe. I'd never seen an eggplant in Australia and grabbed the closest thing handy to write the ingredients and method. I still have the side of that Tampax box, scrawled with my rushed scribble, pasted into my recipe book.

I was now a stone lighter than when I left Adelaide 18 months earlier. Everyone had lost heaps of weight in Asia, and at one point I'd lost about ten pounds, but it kept creeping back on. At last I was almost my ideal weight. I had my hair cut to shoulder length, which suited me better than the longer style I'd had for a while. I wrote in my journal I felt like a new person. Since those days in Greece, I've managed to keep my weight down. Perhaps four months of stinking hot, dry weather and healthy food finally broke my bad eating patterns of the past. I always think fondly of Greece for saving me from a lifetime of boring dieting.

All the ex-pats tried to learn a bit of Greek, but soon gave up. It was just too far removed from English. Bahasa Indonesia had been a breeze in comparison. Charley told me when he first arrived he'd chatted to an English woman who'd been working in Greece for a few months.

"Can you speak any Greek?" he asked.

"Can anyone?" she shrugged.

It seemed it was easier to learn American. Danny called Donna's son Barbie Jarn, which was pronounced Bobby John in Australian.

One day when the *Zulu Charlie* returned from a charter, I went down to the port sporting my fashionable new jeans and haircut. The deckhand commented on my new appearance. Charley took a second look. "Have you had your hair cut?" he said.

"Charley wouldn't notice if I had my head cut off." I laughed.

I wasn't really upset – I think I fell in love with Charley when he said he thought diets were ridiculous. He never once criticised anything about me in all the time we were together.

*

There were now five of us living in the little flat – me, Danny, Leonie, Melanie and Billy, the nine-year-old son of one of the white American sailors. Leonie had always been kind-hearted and felt for Billy's father as he had split up with his wife and had custody of his son. He needed someone to look after Billy while he was at work, including longer times when he was at sea. So far, he hadn't found a suitable carer. Leonie offered our services as there was always someone around to care for the kids. She'd worked in all sorts of jobs since leaving school at 13, and this was another way to make a bit of money.

Billy teased Danny mercilessly, Danny reacted by screaming, Melanie yelled at Danny to shut up, and she and Billy argued constantly. Leonie, who had linked up with one of the black sailors, Jimmy, spent every night in his flat on the floor below ours. She'd wander back in around lunchtime and organise herself for the night shift at Bobby's.

I was going nuts. I'd chosen to work the afternoon shift so I'd have evenings free when Charley was in port, but being cloistered with three fighting kids wasn't on my agenda. Leonie, rarely there, was oblivious of the dramas. Inevitably it all fell apart – Billy went somewhere else and Leonie got a flat for herself and Melanie in the same block. Peace at last!

Also inevitably, Charley and I had a showdown. The charter season was coming to an end, and so consequently was his job on the *Zulu Charlie*. A yacht bound for the West Indies was looking for crew and we'd both thought about it, but time was against me. I'd have to send Danny back to his grandmother in Adelaide and sell the van. There just wasn't enough time. This wasn't an issue for Charley – if we both managed to organise it, well and good, if not he'd go alone.

"If you go away on that yacht, we won't see each other for six months. I'm not sitting around waiting for you anymore." I was crying tears of frustration. "If you go, we're finished. I won't keep in touch."

Charley was genuinely surprised. "You're blackmailing me," he said.

The universe came to my rescue – I got a letter from the yacht captain saying all the crew positions were taken. Charley headed back to France to deliver the *Zulu Charlie* to its winter home port. He confessed he was actually sick of being at sea and was looking forward to travelling around in the van when he got back to Greece.

The following day, Royce smashed his car.

He was out of action for a few weeks while he slowly recovered and after being discharged from hospital didn't come to Bobby's Bar or the Cave. I decided this was probably just as well and went back to my old routine of caring for Danny and working in the bar. Eventually Charley turned up after travelling for a few days from Antibes. He came in when I was working a late shift and sat drinking for a while, waiting for me to finish. Eventually lack of sleep got to him and he went back to the flat. In the meantime Royce had also turned up, his first night out on the town since the accident.

"Do you want to come to the Cave when you finish?" he asked, all charm and smiles.

Sadly, I had to tell him I was no longer fancy free…

Chapter 17

Overnight, summer changed to autumn – the temperature dropped 10 degrees and stayed that way. Charley, Danny and I set off for London in the van. After four months in Greece I felt the time was right.

I'd only seen two Greek Islands during all our stay there, Corfu and Paros. Charley was keen to go to the island of Skiathos, off the east coast – mountainous, wooded with pines, white sand beaches, whitewashed houses. So much better than Paros in the Cyclades Islands south of Athens where Leonie and I, ignorant of local conditions, had headed with the kids. Nobody had told us about the *Meltemi*, the relentless wind which blows all summer. The Cyclades aren't known as the Windy Isles for nothing. There I found out how draining wind can be. My hair stood at right angles to my head for a fortnight. Skiathos, thankfully, was calm. In Paros, I bought myself a long wrap-around skirt and matching top in a patterned blue cotton. I swanned around feeling trendy. That is, until I washed it. It shrunk six inches. I complained to the vendor, who just shrugged. I handed it down to Melanie, Leonie's daughter, who fitted into it perfectly. She was nine years old. I saw lots of tourists wearing similar outfits they'd just bought. I wondered why the suppliers didn't get the seamstresses to wash the cloth before making the clothes. Most of the outfits wouldn't have been worn again after their first wash. Perhaps they just didn't care, figuring most buyers would be long gone before they found out they'd wasted their money.

We got out the maps and plotted a straight line across Europe from Greece to London. Even though this was just a practical way of getting from A to B, and we weren't planning on a Grand Tour, it was impossible to travel across Europe without experiencing a world so foreign to Australia.

> We headed north to Meteora, a truly fascinating place with strange rock formations rising high into the sky, with weird monasteries built way up in impossible places. We wandered round one, Varlaam Monastery, which is still being used by monks. Stayed at another lake

last night, Lake Kastoria, not far south of the Albanian border. Very pretty with lots of trees. There's a fifth century castle here in Ohrid, overlooking the town. Must try to summon the energy to see it.

It's rained practically non-stop for the past three days, ever since we entered Yugoslavia. The van is pretty wet on the floors, but apart from that not too bad. Hope it stops soon, we're all sick of being stuck inside. After Ohrid, we went south along the shores of the lake to Sveti Naum, right on the Albanian border, but we were seen off by an Albanian soldier – apparently we go too close. We wandered round a monastery there, then back through Ohrid to Prizren where we spent Friday night. It's a really nice town, with the odd few churches built centuries ago. The drive was spectacular through the Dinaric Alps past rivers and lakes, and trees with leaves of all colours covering the mountainsides.

Most campsites seem to have closed on September 30th, so we spent the night parked on the side of the highway. Haven't tried Yugoslav food yet, but their cakes are beautiful, sickly but beautiful. The peasants here wear very colourful clothes – the women wear baggy pants gathered at the ankle, and donkeys are their main form of transport. Horses and carts are used to transport hay, vegetables etc. Not too good in the pouring rain! Got Danny some boots in Prizren – black leather to his calves with zips, and fur-lined. He was delighted with them. One pair of broken thongs and a pair of holey slippers aren't much use in this weather. They only cost $8 US – very cheap.

From there we ambled along through Pec to the Cakor Pass, covered with snow right on the top of the Alps. Beautiful country as always – snow-covered fir trees all over the place. Charley and I had two shots of Slivovitz, the local plum brandy, while Danny played in the snow. Our footwear was hardly adequate – my desert boots and Charley's sandshoes soon were soaked.

Danny came into the warmth of the café. "I've lost my hovercraft," he announced. This was his favourite Matchbox toy, and unfortunately white. We traipsed outside, leaving our half-finished brandy. He led us to a patch of snow and we dug around for a few minutes. My feet were dropping off.

"Are you sure you were playing with it here?"

"No, I was over there," he said innocently, pointing to another patch of snow under a tree.

We left it for a Yugoslav kid to find after the thaw.

The road was a bit dicey – dirt covered with snow and ice. It snowed while we were driving along – lovely soft flakes, no ice or sleet. Spent the night at Morača on top of a waterfall and found dozens of mushrooms that night and the following morning. The countryside was still beautiful – autumn leaves, rugged mountains and steep gorges.

Tonight we are in Budva on the Adriatic Sea. We arrived at the coast at Petrovac, hoping for a bit of sunshine. Some hope, it's still raining now. We've stuck to backroads up to now, but it will be the highway all along the coast.

Yugoslavia has six Socialist Republics. So far we've been through Macedonia, Serbia and Montenegro. Really nice sounding names.

*

Three weeks later we were in Bavaria, in Stuttgart.

"If Ingo behaves like an arsehole, I'm not staying," I told Charley.

We were looking for the home of Ingo and Helen, the couple we got to know in Goa in India a year earlier. Ingo was obnoxious when he'd been drinking. I could still remember an afternoon at their place. Danny had been playing with little Carlie and the room was a mess.

"What have you little bastards been up to?" Ingo laughed as he surveyed the chaos. Danny was sitting on a bench next to the wall. Ingo turned towards him. His fixed grin had always made me uncomfortable. It was a smarmy grimace.

"You *are* a little bastard, you know."

I kept my mouth shut. Helen's life was difficult enough without her friends storming off. I can still picture Ingo, glass of booze in one hand, raving about some rubbish to his captive audience, then toppling sideways off the verandah. It was quite a drop, but unfortunately the village houses were all built on sand.

> Finally located Ingo and Helen in Schwabisch Hall, a lovely little town not far from Stuttgart. Really winding narrow streets with Tudor-type houses. We spent two days with them, very enjoyable surprisingly. Ingo has improved out of sight and Carlie is really a nice little kid now. Did a tour of every pub in the place – Ingo still likes to drink. Also smoked a couple of joints of Ingo's home-grown grass. He told us he plucks the leaves all the time, keeping the plant small and bushy. It must work – it was great grass.

Some things hadn't changed since India.

Surviving the Seventies

*

From Germany we headed in a straight line across France to the ferry at Dunkirk. Watching our money had become second nature, but as we drew nearer to the home comforts of the United Kingdom, we decided to splash out on a final meal in a proper French restaurant.

Mostly we bought local food and I cooked it in the back of the van while Charley read to Danny in the front seat. I felt if I heard *Mr Punnymoon's Train* once more, I'd have a meltdown. Kids' books in English had been thin on the ground and this was his favourite from India. All we had to cook on was a little single gas burner, fuelled by a blue disposable *Le Gaz* canister. I'd cook in stages. One meal was stuffed capsicums. First I'd cook rice, set it aside, then lightly fry diced vegetables and perhaps finely sliced meat. I'd cut the top off the capsicums, stuff them with the filling, put the top back on, wrap each in alfoil and steam them in a saucepan with a bit of water in the bottom. Other times, we'd have spaghetti bolognaise. It wasn't always easy to wash the dishes straight away, depending on where we were camping. I found wiping everything with toilet paper, then stacking it all in our plastic wash basin until we found a tap solved the problem.

I liked cooking and didn't mind doing it all. Charley happily amused Danny and did the dishes.

We had no disputes over domestics. Usually we'd have a glass or two of wine as I got dinner ready. One evening I'd had a few too many and the saucepan tipped off the little gas burner. It was always a bit unstable and had to be watched. I quickly scooped whatever was in it off the metal floor of the van, gave it an extra minute or two on the burner and served it up. Charley and Danny, their backs towards me, remained ignorant of this little culinary drama. There was nowhere to buy any replacement food at that hour of the night. The odd bit of grit I blamed on the fresh vegetables bought at the local market.

We chose a mid-range French restaurant for our final meal in France, made ourselves as presentable as we could with our limited choice of well-worn clothes, and took our seats. I'd done five years of French at school, Charley had done three. He always amused me as he spoke in the present tense in all situations. The menu was entirely in French, unsurprising as the French in general were antagonistic towards the English in those days. Charley chose something familiar but I cast caution to the wind and picked a dish purely because of its name, a bit like picking a horse in the Melbourne Cup. *Andouillette*, what a lovely sound.

The young waitress set our main courses on the white linen tablecloth. "*Bon appetit!*"

What was this in front of me? It looked like a large, fat, pale-coloured sausage, obviously encased in animal intestine, the traditional sausage casing. I tentatively cut it open. Lots of little pieces of translucent intestine spilled on to my plate. Each was about half an inch long. They reminded me of the chicken entrails I'd seen as a kid when my father cleaned one of our chooks he'd just chopped the head off, about the same diameter. On principle I felt I had to try it. One tasteless rubbery mouthful was enough. Charley kindly let me eat a bit of his, barely disguising his mirth. I felt the universe had let me down – I should have been rewarded for my daredevil behaviour.

We lined up in wild weather for the ferry at the Dunkirk wharf, subdued by the thousands of white war graves we'd passed by on the way.

Chapter 18

Back in London we did the usual traveller thing and tried to find people who could put us up. We'd met two Australian girls in Greece and had their address in Hampstead, but alas one was already back in Australia and the other was leaving in two days. Next we drove to Fulham where I'd stayed with my sister Rosemary and her boyfriend nearly a year before. Mark's Kombi was parked outside but the place was deserted. There was a For Sale sign out the front. We walked around the building several times, knocking on doors and windows, but no luck. We had to resort to a Youth Hostel.

I took Danny to the Sudbury Nursery for four days. It gave Charley and me a chance to do a few things alone, such as going to Australia House, the bank, visiting the Planetarium, Harrods and going to see the rock opera Tommy.

Yesterday we set out for the country at last, stopping at Winchester to see the Norman Cathedral, then on to Stonehenge where we stayed the night. Charley pointed out the Barrows where important tribal members were buried. There are lots of ancient sites round Salisbury Plain. We passed Figsbury Ring, a Roman fortification now overgrown, and also Old Sarum, a hill fort from the Iron Age and the earliest settlement in Salisbury.

Today we stopped at Cadbury Castle, believed to be the site of Camelot and visited Horsington and Yeovil, two towns where Charley lived as a child. I'm writing this on top of Ham Hill, a rather weird hill with a series of lesser hills and tracks on top – great for kids to play in. We went to Dorchester, the site of Thomas Hardy's *Mayor of Casterbridge* and saw Hardy's cottage in the woods. A lovely place, with grey squirrels everywhere. We went to a seaside village, Brixham, then headed north through Dartmoor (saw the prison). Very bleak and foggy place, with brown bracken everywhere and lots of Dartmoor ponies. At last I'm seeing some of the places I read about as a kid and now know what holly, gorse, oak trees, chestnut trees etc are all about.

Also drove through Bodmin Moor and saw Jamaica Inn, the setting of Daphne du Maurier's book of the same name. I had no idea it was a real place. As we drove through the drizzling rain it appeared before me, a wonderful dark building in the swirling mist, straight off the cover of her book. It was so surreal, I felt I'd seen a ghost. I literally did a double-take, just like in the movies.

Headed to the north coast of Cornwall to Tintagel, also claimed to be the site of King Arthur's Camelot. Wandered round the ruins of Tintagel Castle, right on the cliffs above the sea. Through Exmoor to Glastonbury where we explored the ruins of the Abbey and also saw the museum where they have artefacts found in the Glastonbury Lake Village, dating from before Christ. Climbed Glastonbury Tor with the remains of an old church still on top.

Drove to Avesbury arriving right at nightfall unfortunately and only saw the outlines of the stones of Avesbury Ring. Spent the night somewhere between Reading and London and arrived back about midday.

Back in London we tracked down Leonie and Melanie who had also driven from Greece in a Kombi Leonie had acquired for the trip. Her brother had stayed in a squat in Islington some time before and even though he'd since moved on, she was welcomed as several of his old flatmates were still there. On the strength of this tenuous link, Charley, Danny and I also moved in.

But major changes loomed.

*

Alone again! Charley and Danny jetted out on the eighth. Can't say I'm really missing them, but that's me and besides I'll be home in a month. I rang home the morning after they arrived and Danny said, "Where you am?" Not so hot on the English, our Danny.

Charley, broke as usual, decided to go back to Australia to work rather than face another English winter. Being British, sightseeing in London wasn't high on his list, but I wanted to stay on a bit and see all the places I'd read about in my childhood and hadn't yet visited. My mother, who hadn't seen Danny for 15 months, happily agreed to have him till I returned. Charley, always Danny's devoted slave, offered to take him back home. I think he was rather looking forward to their trip home together, just the two of them. The only time I can remember Charley getting annoyed with him was once when Danny woke him too early, but when Charley realised it was actually after midday he felt guilty and said he was sorry. Back somewhere in Asia I'd once said I wished Charley was Danny's father.

"I wish I was too," Charley said.

*

The squat in Islington was a three-storey brick building belonging to the council and currently housed about ten people. It had been unoccupied until discovered 12 months earlier by Jarvis and his mate Paul. They'd let themselves in, changed the locks, had the electricity and gas connected, and invited various friends and acquaintances to move in. Once squatters moved in, the lawful owner of the premises had to go through the courts to evict them, but given the backlog of similar cases this process took six months. In the meantime, everyone had free accommodation. After my hideous experience in London a year earlier trying to find a place for myself and Danny, I had no qualms about occupying an empty council property.

It had a huge kitchen on the ground floor, still furnished from the days it was a functioning health-care centre. Most of our socialising was done around the old dark wooden table, cluttered with bottles of beer and wine, tobacco and grass and ashtrays. On the next floor was an equally large living room and a few bedrooms. The top floor rooms were all being used as bedrooms, and both the top levels had a bathroom and toilet. Not bad for free accommodation. One afternoon Jarvis and Paul turned up carrying a sofa they'd found on the side of the road 3 or 4 kilometres away. They carried it back, putting it down on the pavement and sitting on it to have a smoke whenever they felt tired.

Leonie and I, free from the responsibilities of parenthood, shared a room on the top floor. Her daughter Melanie, by then nine years old, had also returned to Australia. She'd never really taken to the travelling life and missed having friends her age to play with and a friend of Leonie's back in Sydney offered to take her until she returned. The friend had a daughter Melanie's age, but they hadn't got on very well before Melanie left Australia and we hoped a year apart might make a difference. Leonie and I went to Heathrow to send her safely on her way. She was travelling as an unaccompanied child with British Airways, the only airline Leonie could find which charged half fare for a solo child. The rest charged full adult fare, reasoning that a hostess would need to pay extra attention. However, at a refuelling stop when everyone left the plane for an hour or two in the airport lounge, Melanie found herself just following the crowd. A hostess noticed her and asked where her parents were.

"I'm an unaccompanied child," Melanie announced, feeling important.

The hostess was horrified. The staff hadn't been made aware of Melanie's solo status, so perhaps the cheap fare was false economy.

When Leonie and I had said goodbye to her as she left the departure lounge, we were clinging to each other in anxiety. Melanie, however, turned and gave a big smile and disappeared down the long corridor into the plane.

*

One afternoon I was sitting reading on the double mattress on the floor of the bedroom I shared with Leonie. She stuck her head around the door.

"Quick, go downstairs. Matthew's in the kitchen."

Matthew Garber, now grown up, was the little boy out of Mary Poppins and friends with one of our flatmates. I was too shy to go. I felt it would be too obvious and I've never been much of an actress. I don't think my mother ever forgave me for this chance to brag to her friends, *Mary Poppins* being one of her very favourite films.

We got *Time Out* magazine as soon as it hit the news-stands and went to lots of plays and films. There were pages of shows on offer. One afternoon we went to see *Dad's Army*. Neither of us had seen the TV series in Australia and knew very little about it. One of Charley's friends from Tasmania who'd visited us in Antibes had seen it and said it was the funniest thing he'd seen in ages. He was entertaining and had a great sense of humour. Unfortunately the show was just about booked out and we had to sit separately. Leonie and I both thought it was dreadful, dated, and with slapstick comedy. We were horrified, not at wasting our time and money, but because we'd told our British flatmates we were going. They'd be laughing at these hick colonials. I hadn't heard of the Cultural Cringe before coming to England, but soon became aware of the condescending manner of a couple of the girls in the squat. We'd loved the play *The Journey of Anais Nin*, and praised it up when we got home. The two toffs took themselves off to see it but were scathing when they returned. Leonie made an effort in our defence.

"Our taste obviously isn't as developed as yours," she said.

I looked daggers at her in an effort to shut her up, but perhaps she was being sarcastic.

All the London places we'd read about or seen on TV were coming alive to us.

We met Gaye, our workmate from Bobby's Bar in Greece, last night at Sloane Square Tube and went along Kings Road to a wine bar then had dinner at the Chelsea Kitchen, a great place. It was lovely seeing her again, she's such a nice girl. We've also eaten out at Cranks, a health-food place near Carnaby Street. Went to Portobello Road last Saturday and got an Indian dress and shirt. Great gear there. Saw Cat Stevens at the Hammersmith Odeon, brilliant to see him live after playing *Tea for the Tillerman* a couple of thousand times on my little cassette player in Asia.

We had a really nice Christmas with most of the house here for midday dinner. Jarvis, Paul, Marianne, Oz, Willie, Chris, Leonie and I had roast chicken, vegetables, plum pudding, wine, whiskey and cider. I was suffering from a hangover as we'd spent the previous evening at one of the local pubs and then I came home and smoked hash with tobacco – always a mistake. We went back to the same pub later Christmas afternoon and enjoyed ourselves until Willie got himself involved in a brawl and ended up with a broken jaw.

I started hanging around with Jarvis. He was about three inches shorter than me, skinny with very white skin and red curly hair to his shoulders, none of which bothered him at all. He was a real charmer with a typical English sense of humour. We spent most of our time together laughing. About this time Charley wrote saying he'd decided to stay in Tasmania and teach. Once more he'd made plans just for himself, not mentioning our vague discussions about moving back to Sydney after we'd spent time with our families.

I knew I should break off our relationship. Why didn't I demand that we talk about our future together? Perhaps I felt if I insisted on laying our cards on the table, he'd back off and finish with me. Maybe the conservative attitudes of the day that men should make all the decisions was just too deeply entrenched. Who was I kidding? There was no point soul-searching. The truth was I instinctively understood the rules of our relationship. He did what he wanted, I fitted in around his plans and if I insisted on us making plans together, we were finished.

The indifference I always felt towards him when we were apart widened, but as always I was attracted towards unlikely guys – first Royce in Greece, now Jarvis who'd spent the odd stretch in prison for falsifying prescriptions. I told myself I was looking for a new guy, but without a definite break with Charley perhaps I subconsciously chose impossible partners. And as always, I chose a guy who dabbled in drugs, but everyone in my circle did then.

At last I've been introduced to acid. I wish I'd had some ages ago, but India was the only place any was available and there was no-one to mind *le petit*. Jarvis and I had some together just before New Year. I found the effect very like the magic mushrooms of Bali, and became very happy and talkative. We stayed up all night and finally went to sleep about 8 am. I feel very warm towards Jarvis – he's very sensitive and sweet and affectionate and seems to live in a different world altogether. I hallucinated only slightly – the walls waved around a little. As usual I need more than most people to get off, and taking a whole tab in two parts with an interval between wasn't enough to get me going.

Leonie, Jarvis and I dropped some more a couple of nights back and really had the full effect. Waving walls, weaving colours, the X-ray effect when staring into your hand. Marie, Bill, Jan, Nick and Fred came up with a cup of tea which was lovely. We had such a euphoric feeling. Bill's face was absolutely beautiful when he spoke. We laughed and laughed and could hardly stop.

Jarvis was lying next to me on a mattress on the floor and it was pretty dark. He was apparently trying to tickle my ribs but misjudged his position and said, "Good heavens, I'm seducing a flock mattress." He paused for a moment. "And what's more, I'm getting a response."

I was incapable of talking for about 10 minutes.

*

January 10th was approaching fast, the day I'd fly out of London, pretty much a year to the day since I'd arrived. I started panicking – there were still places on my list I had to see. Jarvis, Paul and Ian took me to St Paul's and the Tower of London. I'd never be able to confess back home I hadn't seen them.

> Sold my rotten van for £30 to a dealer. Apparently it was very rusty in the chassis and would have cost a couple of hundred to fix it. That's life, and it's only money! Jarvis gave me his leather wristband as a going-away present, and Paul his set of Carlos Castaneda books on Don Juan. Leonie mulled some wine with brandy in it so it was a really nice going away. Marie and Nick came up to say goodbye. Marie's so sweet, I must keep in touch. Steve shared his grass with us. A really nice farewell.
>
> Jarvis and Leonie came out to the airport to see me off which was really great of them as we

had to get up at 6 am – a truly impossible task for such a night-orientated house. It's about 2 am in London now as I write so I guess they'll all be getting ready for bed. I felt really sad to leave. I'm forced to admit that I was well and truly settled into their way of life – getting up at 11 or 12, pottering round doing one or two things in the city, coming home and watching telly until tea-time (usually eight or nine pm) then more TV or down to the pub and always plenty of hash and grass. Effing amazing!

And I still have the plaited leather bangle Jarvis gave me when I left.

Chapter 19

In those days the long haul between the UK and Australia was broken by a stopover, usually Singapore or Hong Kong. I'd originally hoped to go via Moscow which was on offer from time to time at the cheap flight centres. For some reason this flight was illegal but still available between crackdowns. Flights were heavily regulated in those days and there was little competition allowed. A couple of weeks before I was due to leave, Moscow was off the agenda again.

The cheapest flight I could find with my shonky student card delivered me back to Singapore. It seemed a lifetime since I'd last been here with Danny en route to Nepal to meet Charley. As the plane approached, my mind wandered to a festival we'd seen back then, coming from one of the temples. Walking along the street came a colourful throng, all gongs and incense and waving banners. In the middle were four or five young guys each with a metal pole about six feet long and half an inch in diameter piercing right through one cheek, through their mouth and out the other cheek. I was so close I could have touched them. They held the pole steady with a hand either side, a helper standing by in case they stumbled. The flesh appeared pierced, I could see the hole where the pole entered, but there was no blood. Were they in a trance? I'd seen trance dancers in Bali, so perhaps this was how they did it.

I found out later that in Singapore, facial piercings are performed during the Hindu festival of Thaipusam, commemorating the god of war, Lord Murugan. However, this is also done there in Chinese temples so I never knew which I'd seen. Apparently the wounds heal without a scar.

> We flew south of Singapore to make our approach and got a great view of the southern islands before landing. Got a taxi for $35 Singapore to the Peony Mansion, where they have dormitories on the fifth floor for $5.50S. Much more sociable than a hotel room, not to mention cheaper. I'm sharing a room with five guys, in fact I'm the only girl here at the moment among a dozen or so guys. I've been

chaperoned everywhere. One of the English guys here has decided he fancies me unfortunately as he's rather a bore. No end of sex-starved males on the Hippie Highway.

It's taken me several days to get over the flight, my cold, and the lack of sleep I had in London, in fact today is the first day I've felt really good. Been eating the usual papaya and pineapple as I wander the streets.

*

When I landed back in Adelaide in the middle of January 1976 I had no idea it would be my home base for the next 22 years.

I caught a taxi to my family home at Kingston Park, on the coast about 20 kilometres south-west of the city. No-one was there, but I let myself in, the house unlocked as it always had been in my childhood. The suburb had originally been called Marino but was renamed when I was about 12. Nearby Kingston House was the home of a former Premier of South Australia, Charles Kingston, who introduced the vote for women in 1894, the second in the world after New Zealand. However South Australian women were the first in the world to actually vote as their next election was due before New Zealand's. Our home had been their coachmen's cottage. I thought Kingston Park pretentious, and kept on saying I lived in Marino.

About half an hour later my mother's little green VW Beetle pulled into the drive. I concealed myself in the dining room and waited until mum and Danny came in the back door, carrying bags of shopping. I stuck my head around the doorway.

"Oh Pammy!" my mother said, obviously delighted. Danny hid behind Mum and peered at me from behind the folds of her skirt. It had only been six weeks since he'd left London with Charley, but he looked different. Perhaps it was just that his hair had grown longer and now curled down below his ears. He seemed taller. When he spoke, his voice seemed higher-pitched. What a lot of changes in six short weeks.

*

After an absence of five years I was home again. When I'd left, South Australia was just beginning to blossom under the premiership of Don Dunstan. When I came back, it was in full bloom.

I was born into conservative politics, both state and federal. The Liberal and Country League led South Australia until I was 16, and the Liberal Country Party governed the whole nation until I was 23. Their very names shrieked caution. Conservatism flowed through our veins.

Young and charismatic, Dunstan's energy and enthusiasm transformed the state. *Women's Day* described him as "the sexiest political leader in Australia". The pink shorts he wore to parliament stunned the Adelaide Establishment, the female members of which we referred to as the "Blue Rinse Set". Dunstan was a reformist and visionary. On his watch, known as the Dunstan Decade, Aboriginal Land Rights were established and he appointed the first Indigenous Governor. He decriminalised homosexuality and abolished the death penalty. Public health and education were improved. Universal suffrage was introduced and the voting age lowered to 18, partly in response to National Service. The 20-year-old guys, unable to vote, were powerless to avoid Vietnam. The physical state of the planet was largely ignored worldwide, but Dunstan created a Ministry for the Environment, perhaps inspired by living in the driest state in the driest continent.

In Australia, Adelaide is considered the arts capital, and hosted the first Festival of Arts in 1960. Dunstan is credited with reinvigorating the social, artistic and cultural life of South Australia and his name is forever linked with the arts and multiculturalism. The Adelaide Festival Centre was built on the banks of the River Torrens at a fraction of the cost and time taken to build the Sydney Opera House. And it was the first to open.

Amidst all this action, *Don Dunstan's Cookbook* hit the bookshops…

I was delighted with the changes. What a welcome home present. I picked up immediately on the new energy. The cloak of staid conservatism had gone forever.

Charley asked me to come down to Hobart, and sent me half the fare. We hadn't seen each other for a couple of months but there was none of the usual distance I felt when we'd been apart, and we had a close, warm time in the week we spent together. But Charley was still Charley, still planning his life at sea on yachts in the Caribbean and the Mediterranean.

I settled in Adelaide, Charley in Tasmania. We were better friends than lovers.

Chapter 20

Back in London, I'd enrolled in both Macquarie University in Sydney and Flinders University in Adelaide, hedging my bets. After a couple of weeks with my family, I started to pack to return to Sydney. I'd loved living there before I went travelling, despite all the dramas of my life then. But as the day passed, my packing became slower and slower. My old Sydney friends had all left, following their own paths, and the doubts I had of finding accommodation for myself and Danny, and childcare, before the university year started in a couple of weeks started to gnaw away at me. I didn't want to miss the first week of lectures because we had nowhere to stay. My dramas in London had forever conditioned me against homelessness. I started to unpack. Since then, I've found that if I make a decision to do something, and set out on that path, it soon becomes obvious if the decision is the wrong one. Maybe my guardian angel blocks my way as I set out on the wrong road.

I enrolled in an Arts degree at Flinders, doing Asian History, Indonesian and Psychology. For this opportunity I could thank yet another Labor politician, Gough Whitlam. Whitlam led the Federal Labor Party to victory in 1972, after 23 years in opposition. *It's Time* was Labor's election slogan, and indeed it was. I had never known anything but Liberal Country Party politics – staid, conservative, pro-monarchy. I was born in the year Labor lost power, a whole generation before. I can still hear Bob Menzies' booming voice and picture his bushy eyebrows.

Overnight Australia changed. Gough bulldozed through with his social reforms, two of which particularly favoured me. The Supporting Mother's Benefit allowed me to be with my son in his pre-school years. Free university education opened doors which had been permanently closed to all but the rich or very smart. I could never have afforded to pay uni fees.

Danny and I stayed in the family home while I got enough money together to rent a place of my own. At least, that was the plan. My mother, who had happily cared for her grandson for six months of my overseas trip and who had been delighted to see me when I came home, had changed. I was bemused by her irritability; my very presence seemed to annoy her. I felt an interloper in my own home.

One day I offered to do the family washing, no mean feat since Mum still had an old green Simpson washing machine replete with wringer. Clothes were washed automatically in the big tub and then fed by hand through the wringer into a trough of rinsing water. Engrossed in my work, I'd hung out the first load and was halfway through the second. I rinsed the clothes in the trough and pulled out the plug to drain the sudsy water before rinsing them a second time. I'd been aware of my mother hovering around the laundry, surprised she didn't use the hours she normally spent washing to do something more interesting.

As the last of the water drained out of the trough, Mum came up behind me.

"Are you going to rinse these twice as well?" she asked aggressively, pointing into the trough. She'd obviously observed me double-rinsing the first load of washing. I jumped at her abruptness.

"Yes, there's still a lot of suds in them," I answered innocently.

My mother fumed. She'd been brought up on a farm in the mid-north of South Australia and water was strictly rationed. I had no idea she only ever rinsed the clothes once. Or perhaps I was an imposter, taking over a role that had always been hers.

It took a while for the penny to drop, that this was the way things were now. I was back to my teenage self, being constantly criticised. In those days, it was because I wasn't doting on my boyfriend, Anton, in the manner my mother thought I should be.

Men were put on pedestals back then, and women were in no way their equals. Very few women worked outside the home and were expected to be devoted caregivers, putting all their own hopes and dreams and ambitions on the back burner, while pandering to those of others. My mother embraced these values with a vengeance, her devotion by far and away outstripping that of her peers.

Perhaps my mother's role as a rescuer started in her twenties when she trained as a nurse, a job she loved. There she met her first serious boyfriend, who was blind. Her next relationship was with a soldier, very ill with TB. He died four months after they married. Undeterred, her third and final relationship was with my father, also a soldier, also suffering from TB.

"Do you see a pattern emerging here?" my sister-in-law remarked.

Once Mum delivered the perfect non sequitur. "I'm no women's libber," she proudly announced. "Give me a good strong man to lean on."

Danny was the new male in my life. My mother was in a state of constant agitation when it became clear I wasn't going to wait on him hand and foot. "I'm worried about your relationship with Danny," she fussed. "I'm always running in while he's watching TV to see if he wants something to eat or drink."

Years later I confided in a friend who happened to be a counsellor. "Your mother has rabidly right-wing, anti-female, pro-male values," she announced.

Well!!! I wouldn't have put it quite like that...

*

History repeated itself. I'd left home at 20 because I was sick of being judged, tired of being in a goldfish bowl. This time a few short weeks after returning home from England I was out the door, never ever again to live in the home of my childhood. Sadly, the chasm which had re-opened between me and my mother never properly closed. In the past, even though we'd had real barneys it all blew over, but this time the wedge remained. When Danny was a baby, mum had visited me twice in Sydney with my youngest brother and sister and stayed a couple of weeks each time. I'd loved having them, and they loved coming to stay. We had a pretty normal family relationship back then.

Perhaps because I was now older and much more street-savvy, I was no longer prepared to take criticism. I'd had enough from Danny's father to last a lifetime. Perhaps my mother's anxiety over my brother had become a permanent fixture and coloured her world.

Perhaps she'd had enough of parenting, and didn't want to be responsible for her grandchildren any more. She never said, and I never asked. When I was growing up, if I disagreed with something she'd said or done, mum called me "an argumentative little cuss". Our family had no tradition of talking through opposing opinions, and neither of us had any insight into the benefits of counselling. No-one had even heard of counsellors back then. It was years before talking about your problems to a complete stranger became mainstream.

Like most women of her era, my mother had dreamed of the white picket fence, falling in love, having a family and living happily ever after, but with a sick husband, five kids and very little money, most of the responsibility fell on her shoulders. She was on the go from morning to night – the housework, shopping, cooking, sewing, gardening and childcare were never-ending. My memory is that she always seemed to be trotting around the house, never walking. Despite all this, she seemed to enjoy her role and rarely complained – but underneath it all she must have often been anxious, especially after becoming a mother for the last time aged 45. It was then that I felt something shift in our family.

I sometimes wondered if my mother needed someone to vent her frustrations on, a scapegoat…

One of my friends, a left-wing artist from a well-heeled Adelaide family, had similar problems with his mother who utterly disapproved of the way he made his living.

"She goes round the house with a mouth like a cat's arsehole," he said.

The artist put his energies into the creative process and eschewed the daily tedium most of us had to cope with. He had a studio in North Adelaide which helped him avoid the many distractions of the sharehouse he lived in nearby. I dropped in one day.

"Come in, come in." He held the door open wide. "I've just been scouring the floor looking for roaches to make a smoke. Avoidance behaviour."

While he put on the jug for coffee I wandered around the studio and admired a watercolour of an old country farmhouse in the lower north of South Australia, so familiar from my many trips there.

"I've been selling limited edition prints of that one. I was keeping track of the numbers in a notebook," he told me with a grin. "But I lost it so I just took a stab in the dark and guessed how many I'd already sold."

"So two Adelaide people now have 'Country Farmhouse 27/50'". I put on my disapproving parent voice.

"Well, yes, quite likely." By now the grin was spreading from ear to ear.

He got a contract to illustrate a company calendar and was given a few complimentary copies when they came back from the printer, sending one to his friend Lee for Christmas. Lee was Adelaide Establishment and raised accordingly. He sent a little thank-you note. "Well done old chap. You haven't lost your touch. And by the way, I thoroughly agree with you. October has always been far too long."

Chapter 21

The atmosphere at home soon had me rushing around looking for a house to rent. I checked out the local real estate agents and found a house which was available until the end of the year. Perfect. It was in a quiet street in Sturt, a suburb near the university, with three bedrooms, orangey wall-to-wall shag pile carpet (it was the seventies after all) and a big backyard. The current tenant, also a single parent, had just bought a place of her own, and wanted to break the lease. The agent could hardly refuse me because I was a solo mother.

It was a sign of the times that although I'd arrived back from my travels absolutely broke I'd managed in a few short weeks to save enough from my Supporting Mother's Benefit to pay the bond and two weeks' rent for a three-bedroomed house. I shared with my brother Bruce's girlfriend for a while, then with two students from Flinders. Rent in Adelaide was so cheap that I could pay all my household expenses and still have enough for a social life.

Back in the UK, I'd asked Danny if he wanted to stay in London or go back to Australia. This created a terrible dilemma.

"In Adelaide there's Nana…" he pondered, "but in London there's the Queen's Guards…"

I'd taken him to see the Changing of the Guard in the dead of an English winter. Even seeing the soldiers dressed in their sombre grey great-coats in the drizzle didn't prevent a fascination with all things military taking hold there and then at the age of four. He became an obsessive collector, first of toy soldiers, then militaria and military history books, and eventually joined the army – twice. He did one stint from 17 to 21, quit to go travelling, then re-joined when he had a wife and step-daughter to support. He now has a huge double garage which the family car has never had the slightest chance of entering – it's crammed with military artefacts worth a small fortune. And all because of a visit to Buckingham Palace…

When I decided to go to uni I'd written to my mother from Europe to let her know. I'd thought she'd be pleased – she'd previously said she'd always wanted one of her children to go to university, her own education having been so hard won. "I don't know why you want to go to university," she wrote back. "It's boys like Greg who have to work to pay taxes for all the fees." Greg was my eldest brother.

Perhaps because I had already studied to be a laboratory technician she thought I didn't need any more qualifications. Perhaps she thought I should get back to work and start earning money for my and Danny's future. Or perhaps she felt men like my brother were being exploited.

In truth, I had mixed reasons for going. For a while I'd felt my qualifications a bit inadequate, compared with the uni students I'd hung around with while travelling. Charley immediately hit this idea on the head – he was full of admiration for anyone with a leaning towards science, being hopeless himself. I felt my education had been one-sided. I'd liked both arts and science at high school, but we were pushed towards science, as teaching was the only door open to students who graduated from high school with arts subjects. Dabbling in the arts now would balance the scales.

Also I was dubious about getting another laboratory job before Danny started school. It was a conservative profession and part-time work was unheard of. I didn't want to get back into the frantic rush from home to childcare to work I'd had when Danny was a baby.

I thought I'd feel old and out of place starting university at 26. It had been traditional to go straight from high school, aged 17. However I found out I was the average age of a first year student at Flinders Uni so things were changing quickly after Labor's free education policy. It was all very strange. I hadn't written an essay since high school, and footnotes were unknown territory. I conscientiously attended every lecture and tutorial, not wanting to get behind and find myself floundering.

Like most universities, Flinders covered a huge area, sprawling across low rolling hills south of Adelaide. The childcare centre was a long way from the lecture theatres and only cared for the kids during the actual lecture and tutorial times. As soon as my class finished, I raced along the path to the centre. Hefty fines were imposed for lateness. There were far too many kids for the places available and two mornings a week Danny had to go to a commercial childcare centre some distance away. Without a car, this involved a lot of rushing on public transport. After a few short weeks of this I realised this set-up wasn't working and enrolled him full-time in the suburban centre. A lot more expensive, but life was easier. Childcare was lagging behind Gough's new education policies.

I was in my mid-twenties and newly single. Like all young singles at uni, I threw myself into the social life. In those days as soon as you split with one partner, you were expected to go on the prowl for another. Being single by choice was unheard of. There was the Tavern, recently opened and full of friendly faces. I joined the Scuba Diving and Horse Riding clubs. Political clubs supporting various local and exotic causes were thick on the ground. I'd been following the misfortunes of Portuguese Timor and joined the East Timor Support Group. Every weekend there was a party to go to, most often more than one. The weight I'd lost in Greece hadn't crept back on. I wore my red patterned Indian wrap-around skirt together with a black skivvy, and boots I'd got in Yugoslavia. My unruly hair couldn't be tamed – wild curly perms wouldn't be in vogue for a couple of years. I developed a crush on Chris Matthews, his Anglo name belying his Filipino roots. Tall, gorgeous with long, thick, straight black hair... predictably I was one of a long line of admirers. Chris was very active politically and had an "Israel is Occupied Palestine" sticker on the side of his bag.

One of the guys in the circle I hung around with related a tale as we sat drinking in the Tavern after classes. "Chris was sitting in here yesterday," he told us, grinning broadly, "expounding his latest political theory. He had two or three young girls hanging on his every word, looking up at him with eyes like puppies." The storyteller leaned back in his chair, his head rolling back as he laughed. "He was totally oblivious of the effect he was having. 'Oh Chris, I've never thought of it like that before,' one of them said." His falsetto re-enactment of the girl's devotion had us all laughing.

However, I did spend a bit of time with Chris, brought together by our political interests, but it became obvious he was still pining for his old girlfriend who had left him a few months earlier. Why was I always attracted to guys who had women dripping off them? It never occurred to me to go for Mr Normal with suit and briefcase.

My old neighbour Ross Ryan, the rock singer of "*I Am Pegasus*" fame, was doing the uni concert circuit and performed at Flinders during the winter. We caught up after the show – it was three years since we'd last seen each other in Sydney and there was a lot of gossip to swap. Our little community in Pennant Hills was no more – the big household where Danny and I had lived had disbanded, and Ross and his girlfriend had left the adjoining cottage. Their menagerie had included a horse Winston, Henry Miller the dog who shared the girlfriend's surname, a cat called Barbara and a sheep which shared the horse-paddock. They all moved to a small acreage which Ross and his girlfriend eventually bought, but they'd since split up.

Surviving the Seventies

*

In mid-winter Flinders University Scuba Diving Club headed off to Yorke Peninsula. South Australian seas are cold at the best of times; in winter they're freezing, and they're also the breeding ground of white pointer sharks, but it never occurred to us this wasn't ok. I hitchhiked across with one of the other girls from the club, our lift having fallen through at the last moment. We pitched our tents on the coast near Troubridge Hill right on the heel of the peninsula but had a very cold night as we'd had to ditch our second sleeping bags, among other luxuries, when we found we didn't have our own transport. I ended up wearing all my clothes to bed, but was still cold. Someone lent me a space blanket but condensation collected under it, making my sleeping bag damp. We dismissed this annoyance and sat closer to the campfire.

"Why did you decide to learn to scuba dive?" one of the guys in the club asked me as we waited for the billy to boil.

"Because I used to watch *Sea Hunt* when I was a kid," I answered.

He laughed. "I knew you'd say that. That's why we all took it up."

Sea Hunt, starring Lloyd Bridges, was an American TV series from the sixties where the sea was always clear, calm and blue.

The following afternoon, dressed in black wetsuits, we huddled on the shore of Troubridge Hill where the sky and sea were steel grey, with a rolling swell sending waves breaking on the shore. I volunteered to go in with the first group, more to get it over and done with than out of any enthusiasm. Scuba divers didn't wear life jackets as in those days a thick rubber wetsuit was considered buoyant enough, and our tanks were only half-full of air as we'd done a short dive earlier in the day. It was late in the afternoon and the club had no support boat. I was paired up with another novice diver who had also only done four sea dives. We waded tentatively into the grey water, submerged, and headed out to sea.

After about five minutes I signalled to go up and check where we were but when we broke the surface the shore was hundreds of yards away – we'd been carried out by a current. My buddy looked towards the beach so far away. "Shit," he said.

We had a brief consultation and decided to head back in, swimming on the surface, but after a few minutes we'd made no ground at all and realised the current had us well and truly in its grip.

We descended to the sandy bottom but the current was still so strong. As the sea surged towards the shore we swam as hard as we could, then dug our fingers in when the sea surged back. Sand and seaweed swirled past us limiting our visibility to a few feet. There was nothing to hang on to, and we frequently lost what ground we'd made when the current dragged our fingers out of the sand. I tried not to think about what we'd do if we ran out of air. Little by little we made headway, and eventually reached the rocky bottom about 100 yards from the shore. Every time the breaking waves pulled back we clung to whatever lump of rock we could hang on to, to stop ourselves being dragged back out to sea. It was worse nearer the shore with the waves breaking over us.

I grabbed my buddy's hand in terror, panic-stricken. He was in no better state than me, but at least we were together. *I can't die like this*, I thought, *My mother can't be left to bring up Danny by herself.* I kept that thought in my head like a mantra as the water and weeds streamed past me. By grabbing the rocks and clinging on when the sea surged back and swimming for our lives when the waves rolled in we eventually staggered ashore.

We knew nothing about rips. Adelaide is in a gulf and there's no surf. Unless there's a storm, the sea is always calm and ideal for swimming so none of us had experience battling currents. But this current seemed to affect the whole of the beach – all eight divers got caught in it and were spread over a large area. Everyone eventually struggled back in. For the third time in my life I thought I was going to die, and the other three novices all felt the same. The more experienced divers said they were confident of getting back to shore, but I thought this was just bravado.

In time I felt grateful for this lesson the sea taught me that day, and have had a very healthy respect for the power of the sea ever since.

*

At Flinders it was impossible to avoid politics. Left-wing clubs abounded supporting Palestine, China, East Timor, Vietnam… the Young Liberals were sailing against the tide. There were rallies and street marches to attend, and fundraising dances for various causes.

I'd been raised in an apolitical household, had my eyes opened a bit in Sydney, saw a lot more in Asia, the UK and Europe, and now was in the thick of left-wing politics in Adelaide. Street marches were common. I joined the Adelaide branch of the Campaign for Independent East Timor (CIET) and marched along King William Street carrying placards behind huge banners, chanting "Indonesia Out Now" through the loud-hailers.

I have a photo from a rally in support of teachers. I'm wearing my blue denim bib and brace overalls, reading a hand-out. Two women, similarly dressed, stand either side of me. Danny is up a tree behind me, looking over my shoulder. Halfway out of my pocket hangs his Action Man toy, naked-chested with bulging muscles. I always smile when I think of the contrasts in that photo.

Fundraisers for East Timor were held in the cafeteria of the University of Adelaide. Supporters would turn up early to hang banners and placards, deliver food and drinks, set up tables near the door to collect the entrance fees, and clear the stage for the band. My left-wing artist friend with whom I shared difficult mother issues designed posters which we pasted up around the city a couple of weeks before the event. I can still picture one of them – a huge colourful butterfly in flight with a strand of black barbed wire across the middle. Occasionally we were accosted by the police who took our names but then did nothing.

Robyn Archer regularly performed at these dances. She went on to become internationally acclaimed, singing rock, blues, jazz and cabaret. The venue was always packed and rocked on into the night. The money raised was used for the basic running expenses of the campaign – printing, telephone etc, and also to fund various speakers, including Chris Santos and Jose Ramos Horta who had both left East Timor before the Indonesian invasion.

I remember Georges and his wife and daughter, East Timorese who had left before the invasion as his daughter needed medical attention in Australia. He had a little dog which he brought to various campaign gatherings. He told me of his sadness at leaving their family dog standing on the wharf in Dili watching them as their boat pulled away.

Chapter 22

Through CIET I met Jo Darke, an Adelaide left-wing political activist. A picture of her being belted by a police truncheon had adorned the front page of *The Adelaide Advertiser* at the height of anti-Vietnam war marches. Jo was an imposing presence, nearly six feet tall with long straight blonde hair, resembling the singer out of Peter, Paul and Mary. She was a skilled speaker and organiser. It was nothing to her to arrange venue, advertising, band, sound system, food, drink, decorations, helpers… we became a well-oiled team. Although Jo had a stack of academic qualifications, she had the gift of explaining complex issues in an engaging way and often took to the stage, addressing huge crowds on various social and political issues. Four decades later, we are still close friends.

*

Jo and I loaded up her old Ford sedan and sped out of Adelaide. It was a couple of days after Christmas 1977 and we were on a month-long road trip. I'd just finished my second year at Flinders and Jo was on leave from her job as a tutor at the Aboriginal Task Force at the Institute of Technology. The back seat was crammed with gear and Matsu, Jo's kelpie-bull terrier-dingo cross, hung his head out the window as we drove away from her cottage in Stepney. He was named after Mr Matsumoto's General Store in Broome, where Jo had acquired him as a pup on a previous trip in the same car. For a pup born into an Aboriginal camp in the north west of Australia he'd come a long way.

This was to be an escape-from-reality trip for both of us. Jo had broken up a while ago with her partner of six years, and I'd just parted with my latest boyfriend, James, Charley's replacement, after a few tumultuous months together. I was still a slow learner. Even after Royce in Greece and Jarvis in London, I was still being sucked in by charm. And like Royce and Jarvis, James was not long-term, happily-ever-after material. Jo and I both needed a lot of space between us and Adelaide. Our plan was to follow the coast south from Adelaide into Victoria, up into New South Wales and southern

Queensland, before returning to Adelaide by the inland route.

My mother, despite our differences, offered to care for Danny who was now five. Did she offer because she thought I needed a break from the demands of full-time study and single parenthood? Did she really want the responsibility of a young child for a month during the school holidays, or was she doing it out of a sense of duty? Did she feel she could indulge my son while I was away and make up for my shortcomings? I'd felt since I'd come back to live in Adelaide she was over the whole childcare bit. Her manner towards me was still disapproving – perhaps she resented that my single parent status had cast her into the back-up role. Or perhaps underneath it all she thought I should stay home and care for my son like a real mother.

I was thankful for the help my mother gave me by caring for Danny, but I felt I was in a cap-in-hand situation, forced into relying on favours. It put my mother in a position of power over me; I could never be independent of her as long as I needed her help. I was caught in the perfect trap. I envied my friends with relaxed relationships with their exes, parents, and in-laws. Dropping Danny off into a house which welcomed me, being met with a friendly smile, would have seemed like heaven. The old saying "It takes a village to raise a child" rang true. Families seemed to be shrinking. I knew lots of single parents, many of them from interstate, and it struck me as a backward step that so many kids didn't grow up in an extended family.

*

In Melbourne Jo and I stayed with an old friend of mine from Sydney days, Yvonne, and her young daughter Su-San who was Danny's age. Su-San's father had been heavily into Zen Buddhism when she was born. We'd been part of a big social group of single parents back then. Yvonne was the first of that group I was hoping to catch up with on this trip. It was now four years since I'd left Sydney, and we'd all scattered. Yvonne was still her laidback self. Even though she'd been estranged from her very religious family since Su-Si's birth, she just got on with it and had a new man in her life, a few years older than her and devoted.

"How's Su-Si's face?" I asked. Yvonne led me to her bedroom. I leaned over and checked the scar on the sleeping girl's cheek. As a toddler, she'd been running through my kitchen at Mosman with a mug I'd been given for my 21st. She fell and the mug shattered against her cheek bone, leaving a deep sickle-shaped cut. Yvonne rushed her to hospital where the gods were smiling – a plastic surgeon had just finished his shift and was getting ready to leave. The scar had always been neat, but red. Yvonne had been assured it would fade and indeed it had – it now followed the line of Su-si's chubby cheek and I could see it would be barely visible in time.

Most people loosen up when driving together for hours and Jo and I found out a lot about each other as the miles sped by. She talked about her former partner who I didn't know as they'd parted before she and I met. Even after more than a year she was still devastated.

"It was like we were in a storm and got parted and couldn't find each other again."

I had always been a good listener, genuinely sympathetic to my friends' woes. I offered the occasional piece of advice, but mostly listened. Two or three times I slipped in something about my problems in my relationship with James, best described as ill-fated, but I already knew how that would end.

Jo contributed steadily to my political education. I learned about animal testing for the medical and cosmetic industries, and female circumcision, two issues I was totally ignorant of. My understanding of the Vietnam War was clarified, and the World Bank and the International Monetary Fund explained. We walked through dense temperate rainforest at Apollo Bay on the Victorian coast – Jo, an environmentalist before the word was invented, was in ecstasies over its beauty, but I must confess my eventual deep appreciation of the natural world was still in its infancy.

We rolled into Sydney on a rainy January afternoon and found my old friend Leonie's Moore Park flat without any trouble. We were soon drinking cups of tea in the cramped little kitchen. It was 12 months since we'd seen each other and there was a lot to catch up on.

Leonie had left school at 13 to work in a butcher's shop in Lithgow, her home town. She was the third of ten kids in a poor Catholic family, and a job was a job. Doctors had recommended that Leonie's mother have a hysterectomy after the birth of baby number nine, but the local priest wouldn't agree. The last baby, a girl, was born with a deformed oesophagus, and died soon after. As would be expected, a lot of family responsibilities fell on Leonie's shoulders. She married young and moved away from Lithgow to another country town, but the marriage was disastrous. After the birth of her daughter Melanie, she escaped to Sydney.

Leonie was very bright and after arriving back in Australia from overseas in 1976, a few months after me, decided to catch up on her education. She was now in her early thirties. Maybe hanging around with all the uni students we met while travelling had a similar effect on both of us. She did years 11 and 12 of high school, then started an arts degree at the

University of NSW. Like me, she discovered a whole new world at university.

My lingering memory of that visit is of Jo's dog Matsu bailing up Melanie's cat on the stairs outside the flat. The only casualty was Jo whose hand was injured when trying to grab Matsu.

Even though it was only four years since I'd left Sydney, all my old friends had gone. Hans and Heather to Nambour in Queensland, my closest single-parent friends Diana to Darwin with her son Sam, David to Nimbin with his son Julian, Yvonne to Melbourne with Su-Si, and my St Ives housemates Angela and Peter to Woolgoolga with their blended family of five kids. Most of us had drifted into Sydney in the early seventies from far afield, and just as easily drifted away. Maybe it was the lack of family ties which stopped us settling. Leonie was the only one left, although she'd been overseas for two years in the meantime.

We spent a few days visiting my old haunts – mostly wine bars and pubs. One favourite, the Bengal Tiger wine bar in North Sydney was gone, burnt to the ground. They called the replacement bar Matches, which makes you wonder. Another watering hole, the Stoned Crow, still exists and is still full of young singles. Not much has changed in 40 years when it comes to looking for Mr or Ms Right, but I hope those today on the hunt have better luck than we had.

A few days later we were north of Coffs Harbour in Woolgoolga, staying in Angela and Peter's weatherboard cottage. A couple of years before, they'd sold the St Ives house where we'd all lived in 1972, piled all the kids in their van and headed north. Angela had never let an insignificant thing like a lack of money stand in her way, and soon opened Angela's Bazaar, a little shop on the beach selling Asian clothing. I was soon in the change cubical, transported back to my hippie days. I still have a pair of long rayon pants I got there. They were originally part of a sky-blue one-piece jump suit. However, once back in Adelaide the beach culture clothing didn't fit in, so I cut off the top and dyed them a darker blue. They've survived so long because they were always too long to wear with sandals and I only occasionally wore heels. I still intend to take up the legs one day...

They'd all taken to the relaxed beach lifestyle. What a change from the stress-filled days in St Ives. They eventually bought a two-storey house right on the beach with just a short wander through bushland to the surf. Peter's daughter eventually joined them, making six kids in total. Angela still lives there with husband number three, a former thoroughbred breeder from the Hunter Valley. Peter lives in Coffs and had two more children with his Filipina partner but they have since parted. The older kids scattered, mostly back to Sydney for study and work.

North of Woolgoolga, we entered the Big River country. First the Clarence, then the Richmond and the Tweed. Jo and I were incredulous. It had never crossed our minds that our own country could have such majestic rivers. In South Australia they were usually dry beds, the Murray being the only big river. A dozen or so turtles were lit up by sunlight while basking on a log in a little side creek. As we drove across the bridge, they all plopped into the water.

My cares fell away as the miles flew by. Whenever I caught myself thinking about James, I deliberately made myself think of something else. It worked. I'd always found distance between me and the former object of my dreams worked wonders. The old cliché was true for me: out of sight, out of mind. Space enough to stand outside the relationship and look back in. I knew from now on, I'd be in control of my life. I should have been a counsellor…

There had been something off about the way James treated me. I once read an article by clothes designer Vivienne Westwood which rang a bell. She was describing her former partner Malcolm McLaren, manager of the Sex Pistols. "I call it jiving with people's emotions. Come close to me and as soon as you're close you'll get pushed away. When you're far away, they'll pull you back. Then they'll get frightened when you get too close."

I'd felt James got a perverse pleasure from playing this cat-and-mouse game.

*

Even back in the late seventies, Byron Bay was a surfing Mecca. Being from Adelaide, Jo and I couldn't surf, but wandered around the headland admiring those who could. It was unseasonably cool and windy, giving us a good excuse not to brave the waves.

When we reached Brisbane, we stopped for a drink in a pub before checking out the nearest caravan park. We got talking to Linda who was about our age with straight blondish hair to her shoulders. She hung out with bikies and invited us to stay when she found out we were on the road. Back in her flat we relaxed with a few beers and soon started chatting. Linda had a black belt in karate. Her family were all karate experts and she'd been learning since she was a kid. She told us how she'd been coming home late one night not so long ago and had been grabbed from behind.

"I don't know what I did," she said, "but he ended up flat on the ground. I ran home screaming and locked myself in. I didn't have a phone so I couldn't call the police. But when I went down to the station the next morning, the police said it couldn't have been serious or else I would have reported it straight away." Her contempt was obvious. "They laughed when I said I was too frightened to leave my flat and didn't have a phone. They weren't interested in taking a statement."

A sign of the times in Joh Bjelke Petersen's Queensland of the seventies.

The TV was on in the background. There had been a child abduction recently and we listened to the latest news. We talked about suitable punishments for paedophiles.

Linda's face turned dark. "Hang them by their balls."

Her reaction, so vehemently expressed, has stuck in my head over the decades.

One of Linda's bikie mates turned up. He wore the uniform – obligatory tatts, jeans and leather jacket – but he was very pleasant and friendly. Perhaps his gang were further down the food chain than the Hells Angels or Banditos.

Our final destination before heading home was Nambour, 100 kilometres north of Brisbane, in the Sunshine Coast hinterland. Ken's old navy friends Hans and Heather lived there. I hadn't seen them since Danny was a baby, six years before. I enquired at the post office in the little town and we were soon bumping along a dirt track to their macadamia nut farm. I was probably the last person they expected to see climbing out of the dust-covered Ford. We were delighted to see each other. Two whippets jumped around our feet.

The wooden framework of their future house stood next to a galvanised iron shed which had been their home for several years. Standing shyly by the door was little Kurt, now three years old. Heather's first pregnancy back in Sydney had ended with a miscarriage at three months. She hadn't been at all impressed when she found out she was pregnant, as they'd already planned the move to Queensland. There was enough to do establishing the macadamia farm, building the shed and starting on the house. But after three months of hideous morning sickness, Heather decided once was enough and that she'd got through the worst of it. Then she miscarried.

Tropical heat, humidity and greenery prevailed at their new home. The little macadamia trees were thriving. We went inside the shed which served as bedroom, kitchen and dining room. What a contrast to their former life in the red brick unit in Epping.

Heather had given away all her winter clothes when they moved from Sydney but the relentless wet season of 1974 had driven them away to Murray Bridge in SA where Hans had been brought up. Heather got a job detailing cars while they waited for the worst wet on record to subside. Fortunately dress standards there weren't high. There was no further news of Ken. Heather had previously written that he'd visited once with his new wife, got upset with them and driven off. That was the last they'd seen or heard of him.

I expected them to be really settled after such a radical change, but they were already looking towards greener pastures further north. They wanted a bigger property. With this in mind, Hans hadn't accessed the home loan he was entitled to after going to Vietnam. He was going to use that for their next house. The current one was being built in fits and starts as the money came in. Jo and Heather were soon talking environmental issues. Heather had become involved with a local group attempting to have nearby rainforest declared a national park. A rare freshwater crayfish lived there. Quite a battle in those pro-development Bjelke-Petersen days.

"You've changed a lot since we last saw you," Heather commented. She was referring to my independence. Her previous impression had been of Ken's dominance. In reality, he'd never truly dominated me. I'd only stayed because I'd had to during my pregnancy, my feelings for him long dead.

Chapter 23

It was time to head home to South Australia. We laid the NRMA Motorists Map of South East Australia on the kitchen table. Our plans were to head straight back to Adelaide.

"This is the most direct route," said Jo, circling Warwick, Goondiwindi, Moree, Collarenebri, Walgett and Bourke. I pored over the map. This was the real outback, the stuff of legends. I still have that tattered old map, the places we stayed marked in blue biro.

When we said our goodbyes the next morning, Hans put his arm around my shoulders and pulled me to him. "It's been good to see you, mate," he grinned. Ken had been his closest friend and it must have been hard for Hans to witness our break-up, followed by the end of their own long friendship established in their navy days so long ago.

We headed inland through Toowoomba and a couple of hours later pulled into Goondiwindi, best known for its champion grey racehorse, Gunsynd. I'd seen Gunsynd at his peak in Sydney when I worked for Sykes and Partners, equine veterinary surgeons. "He got his name when he was first bought at the yearling sales," I told Jo. "When the auctioneer hit his hammer on the final bid he said, 'Sold to the Goondiwindi syndicate.' So he became Gunsynd." I'd done well with all the tips I got from the trainers during my year at the vets. I placed modest bets, and came out well in front.

I was keen to see Moree. My best friend from school days had stayed there on her uncle's sheep property, riding horses and mustering. She and I were both horse mad, and I was most envious. In a funny coincidence, Jo much later had a lot of contact with my schoolfriend's uncle, a keen environmentalist for the local Gwydir River wetlands.

Before we left Adelaide on our trip, Jo had contacted a former student from her days tutoring at the Aboriginal Task Force at the South Australian Institute of Technology, saying we'd be passing through Walgett in late January. The student's mother had recently died, and she'd returned home for a while. I can still see her big smile as we sat on the banks of the

Barwon River which was barely a trickle at that time of the year, next to the remains of a little fire scattered with broken red yabby shells. She told us they occasionally ate echidna and it tasted great. We spent the night in town with her family in their weatherboard home. I wondered how many Aboriginal students actually got to play host to their tutors, particularly one in shorts, with long blonde hair, driving a beat-up, dusty old Ford with a dingo cross hanging out the window.

Reluctantly we changed our plan to go west to Bourke. The road was just too bad. I'd always fancied going "back o' Bourke". Instead we headed straight south and joined the Barrier Highway to Broken Hill. We stayed overnight at a caravan park. Matsu was left tied up there while we went to the pub. He must have got bored. When we got back some hours later, he'd chewed several guy-ropes off the tent. Not just through the ropes, but including large parts of the tent as well. We re-tied the ropes to the tent as best we could. This was doubly unfortunate as it was a borrowed tent from Jo's old share-house. When we got back, she returned it neatly packed. I've wondered on occasion what the reaction was when the next person to use it went camping.

We joined the Barrier Highway at Nevertire which no doubt has an interesting tale to tell.

The height of summer was not the best time to drive through the outback, particularly in the days before air-conditioning in ordinary cars, but because there was no alternative we accepted it as normal to be driving in temperatures of around 40 degrees. We headed due west through Nyngan, Cobar and Wilcannia on the dry Daly River before driving straight towards the setting sun into Broken Hill. Although Broken Hill is in New South Wales, it's close to the South Australian border, much closer to Adelaide than Sydney. Because of this, South Australians consider Broken Hill part of their territory. I'm not sure what New South Welshmen think of this. We spent the night there, before our final push to Adelaide.

As we drove through the mid-north of SA I pointed out places of my childhood. My mother's family farm is at Yatina, a tiny settlement near Peterborough, where we spent all our long school holidays as kids. My great-grandfather had acquired virgin land there in the late 1800s, eventually buying out neighbours to establish a huge property. From the farmhouse, land as far as the eye can see is part of the farm. Massive holdings are required in such dry country, just south of the big cattle and sheep stations.

The farmhouse had a very large kitchen fuelled by a wood stove. Oblivious to the 100 plus Fahrenheit degrees outside, my grandmother lit the stove as soon as she got up each morning, producing sponge cakes, roasts, biscuits, whatever was required for the three main meals and morning and afternoon teas needed to keep the hard-working men happy. My grandparents' bedroom led off from one end of the kitchen, though I never saw them use it. They had a double bed on the back verandah during the summer and preferred the fresh air. Another door off the kitchen led into the lounge. I remember stern portraits of my great-grandparents in dark wooden frames overlooking the evening activities. We played cards, Chinese chequers and ludo, television being decades away in that part of the world.

A door from the lounge led into the second bedroom where my family used to sleep when we visited. My mother was born in this room in 1916. When it was clear the baby was on its way, my grandfather saddled his horse and rode into Peterborough, over 20 miles away, to get the doctor. By the time they returned, my mother had arrived. Not long after, my grandmother Florence, having survived the birth of three children in such a remote location, was badly burnt when a methylated spirits heater exploded. This, along with a chronic kidney condition, led to her early death when my mother was only 14 months old. I have a lot of respect for my grandmother and the difficult life she led, but

I'm not sure that extends to being given Florence as a middle name in her memory...

The children were cared for by their paternal grandmother, but she died when my mother was six. Her place was soon taken by my great-aunt Doris, my dead grandmother's youngest sister, who at 16 wasn't so much older than the children she cared for. After a few years she and my grandfather married and had another son between them. We always called her grandma, Great Aunt Doris being too much of a mouthful. Grandma walked with a limp, having fallen and dislocated her hip as a young child. In those isolated back-blocks of country South Australia in the early 1900s, doctors were miles away and she was left to recover unattended.

Like all the farmhouses back then, the main rooms were sheltered by wide verandahs. My Uncle Bruce had a bedroom at the end of one of these, but like my grandparents he never slept there in the summer. A tarpaulin covered the bedspread of his outdoor bed. The dogs weren't supposed to rest there, but sneaked up when no-one was around. I remember sitting on his bed one afternoon watching a wasp building a mud nest on the wall nearby. It made perfect little round domes of mud, then flew off for a few minutes, returning with a comatose spider or caterpillar which was pushed into one of the chambers. The wasp then laid an egg on the victim before flying off again to get mud to seal the tomb. By the late afternoon the task was finished and a nest the size and shape of an upturned bowl clung to the stone wall. No-one thought to remove it; it was part of life in the country.

A huge gumtree overhung the low stone fence which surrounded the farmhouse. A branch had broken off some time before and left a hollow in the stump still attached to the trunk. A pair of budgerigars made their nest here and I watched them closely as they came and went, feeding their babies. I'd never seen budgies on the farm before – they usually lived in the real desert country further north.

The major attraction for my two brothers and me was the peacock, a splendid creature who displayed his fanned-out tail for all to admire. Summer was his moulting time and we'd try to be the first up in the morning to run around the farm looking for his discarded feathers. When we caught the train back to Adelaide at the end of our holidays we'd all be clutching a bunch of beautiful plumes. He'd been given to my grandmother many years before. He didn't have a mate but hung around with the turkeys during the day. I can still hear his loud, distinctive cry. He nested with the galahs high up in another of the farm's gumtrees, aware of the foxes which patrolled at night, his long tail trailing behind him over the branch. Alas, as he grew older and less sprightly, he took to sleeping on the side of an old hay trolley in the stables, where he eventually met his fate in the jaws of an athletic fox.

At the far end of the verandah alongside the kitchen was a basic bathroom, just a tub with a wood-chip heater. Because of the permanent water shortage, we had a bath once a week, my brothers and I sharing the same water. The toilet was the classic outback dunny, a can under a wooden seat inside a little galvanised iron shelter engulfed in the trailing branches of a huge old pepper tree, a hundred yards or so from the house. You sprinkled ashes from the woodstove once you'd finished. I always held my nose when I paid a visit. I disliked the smell of pepper trees for years, but perhaps that was because of the association.

My eldest brother, Greg, and I went spider hunting one day. We found an old metal enamelled container with a lid and caught spiders by pulling the bark off gumtrees, exposing the creatures to the twigs we used to catch them. One was particularly big, yellowish in colour across its broad flat back. Once in the container, they didn't try to escape but hid in the furthest corners. Greg carried this prize, by now holding a couple of dozen, back home and put it under his bed that night. When my mother was let in on this adventure the next morning she persuaded us to set them free, pointing out that Grandma wouldn't like it if they escaped in the house. My mother was one of the few people I've met without a fear of spiders. Unfortunately, my early bravado didn't last and I became fearful in later years, not helped by the large huntsman my brother and cousin put on my pillow one night.

There was also a pet kangaroo which hung around the farmyard. She was a pretty little creature, a soft grey colour. Once I was playing outside in the sandpit near the water tank and the kangaroo was nearby. I was very young, probably no more than three years old, and threw a handful of sand at her. She took a couple of bounds towards me and placed her two front paws on my shoulders, looking into my face with her round brown eyes. I fled screaming and learned never to throw sand at kangaroos. One day she was a long way from the farmhouse, drinking from a water trough down near the public dirt road which headed north-south, dividing my grandfather's land. Someone driving past shot her, tossed her body in the back of his truck and headed south. My uncle was ill in bed with the flu and couldn't pursue them. It was illegal to shoot on private land, but shooting, usually of rabbits and foxes, was common in the district. However, kangaroos rarely came this far south, making her a hard-to-resist target.

We always spent part of our holiday at my mother's sister's place, a dairy a few miles north of the farm. My Uncle Henry sent us off one day to a nearby paddock to turn the recently harvested sheaves of hay which were piled in stooks, rather like Indian teepees. We ran around pulling these apart so the hot sun and dry air would prevent any mould. Eventually we got to the last stand and began pulling it apart, looking forward to finishing the job and going off to play. Out shot a black snake, across my cousin Kathy's flimsy sandals and then over my bare feet. We ran off screaming. The snake, no doubt equally terrified, secreted itself in a nearby sheaf. This was the second time in my short life a snake had slid across my bare toes, the first being when our fox terrier dug up a brown snake from a hole in the footpath near our front fence, back home in Marino.

Uncle Henry bred trotting horses which he raced at the local country meetings, sometimes taking us all to watch. I was horse crazy and hatched up a plan. I got my brothers and cousins up early and headed for the horse paddock. We enticed Bob, my uncle's two-year-old stallion, over to the fence with a handful of hay. I climbed on the fence-post, placed my bare foot on his back, and slid across. Bob dutifully walked along the fence-line, snatching mouthfuls of hay from Kathy. All my cowboy-and-Indian fantasies were coming true. We kept this up for half an hour or so, taking turns to straddle Bob's broad brown back. The next thing I remember seeing from my perch up high on Bob was my uncle running across the home paddock, yelling. And so ended that particular fantasy. But perhaps my uncle had a point – after all we were riding an unbroken two-year-old stallion, but to us Bob was as quiet as a lamb and just as pleased with this mutually beneficial arrangement as we were. Our future riding escapades were restricted to Dolly, a guernsey cow just as tolerant as Bob, but approved of by Uncle Henry.

My grandfather also loved his horses and had big teams to pull the plough when my mother was young. Every night before going to bed the last thing he did was to walk across the hard-baked ground to the thatched stables, carrying his kerosene lantern to check on his horses. When tractors came in he was one of the first to buy one, but didn't shoot his horses like a lot of his neighbours did. When I was young, his last remaining draught-horse was living out its days in a paddock a long way from the farmhouse. I felt sorry for it as its mates had all died off as the years passed. I wondered why my grandfather didn't bring him closer to the house. One day a solitary sheep was discovered in the paddock with the horse. The public dirt road went past the paddock and perhaps one of the neighbours also felt sorry for the lonely old horse. The two creatures could be seen grazing contentedly side by side. When the old horse eventually died, the sheep was put in with the rest of the flock.

Near the horse paddock was the front gate to the farm, and next to the gate stood a windmill. Digging a well back in the late 1800s was a daunting task. When my grandfather and his brother got home from school one afternoon, they ran eagerly as usual to see how the well was progressing. The little brother stumbled over some tools near the edge and fell into the darkness of the deep shaft. By the time a rope was fetched and my great-grandfather lowered into the well, his son was dead.

"Grandpa never got over his brother's death," my aunt told me. The boys' mother had died some time before, so perhaps they were particularly close.

My grandfather was well over six feet tall with very broad shoulders and thick wavy white hair. He'd pour black tea from his teacup into the saucer, blow on it a couple of times, then sip it from the edge, the ends of his bushy moustache dipping into the tea as he drank. He was very deaf by the time his grandchildren came along, and we were all in awe of him. One day he told us to herd a large turkey gobbler into the fowl yard. Because of his deafness he spoke very softly and we didn't understand what he was saying. When he later saw the turkey still wandering around the yard he sternly asked us why we hadn't done what we were told. Later that night as my mother helped me change into my pyjamas I tearfully told her we couldn't understand what he'd said.

"Why doesn't Grandpa get a hearing aid?" I sobbed.

"He says he doesn't always want to hear everything people say to him," she laughed.

When I was born my father rang the farm with the news of my safe arrival.

"Another lamb in the fold," Grandpa said. I was his second grandchild.

After the dramas of the birth of his own children, my grandfather must have been relieved that hospitals were available for his daughters.

The farm has been in the family for four generations, now farmed by my cousin Frank, who had three daughters before a son was born. It will be interesting to see who inherits the farm.

As the miles flew by as Jo and I headed south, I thought of how lucky my brothers and sister and I were to have experienced so much life in the country, taken so much for granted when we were young.

*

Jo dropped me off at the red brick house in Edwardstown where I'd been living before we set out on our trip.

It was the end of four years of travel and university.

Time to get back into the real world.

Shoutline

Flared skirts, beehive hairdos, stay-at-home mums… Australia in the fifties and sixties was comfortably conservative. Then along came the seventies…

This is the story of how one young Australian navigates her way through a decade of upheaval.

www.ingramcontent.com/pod-product-compliance
Lightning Source LLC
Chambersburg PA
CBHW021142080526
44588CB00008B/172